THE Tell it - Make it BOOK

Author
Shari Lewis

Illustrator
Bozé

Published by
J. P. Tarcher, Inc.

Distributed by
Hawthorn Books, Inc.
Publishers,
New York

Library of Congress Catalog Card # 72-86656

ISBN 0-87477-003-3

Printed in the United States of America

Published by J. P. TARCHER, INC.
9110 Sunset Blvd., Los Angeles, California 90069

DEDICATED TO—

The Girl Scouts of America and
Troop #90 of Beverly Hills, California.

The magic fingers of Mary Litvinoff.

And to my nine-year-old, Mallory Jessica Tarcher,
who has helped me by putting her own books aside
for a moment to read mine and give me her suggestions.

TABLE OF CONTENTS

CHARLIE HORSE'S MAGIC SHOW

STRICTLY FOR THE BIRDS

"HOW-MANY-DAYS-'TIL-CHRISTMAS?

HIDDEN CHRISTMAS TREASURES

MAY I SUGGEST—?

PART 1

The Chiefest Chief and the Bravest Brave

It was a gray and rainy morning. Baby had fallen asleep, sprawled over her Teddy Bear in the playpen, but Lamb Chop, Hush Puppy and Charlie Horse were huddled around Shari as she told them an old Indian story.

As Shari closed the book, Charlie Horse exclaimed, "Say, you know what? I've got the best idea!"

"We won't know that until we hear it, Charlie," Shari teased.

"As long as we have to stay inside today," he continued, "why don't we all play Indians?"

"Oh, yeaaah, ole Charlie Horse," Hush Puppy drawled in his Southern accent.

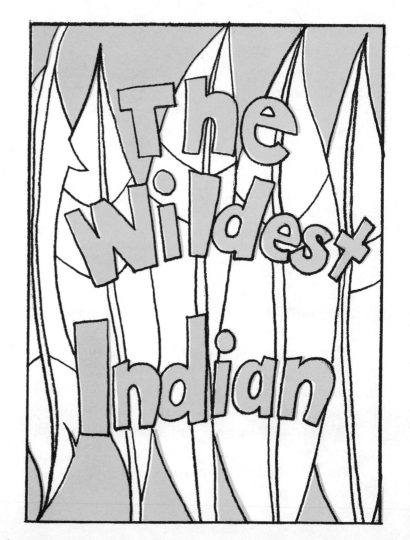

"You *do* have the best idea," said Lamb Chop admiringly.

Shari stood up. "While you're playing Indians, I think I'll go to the store for some ice cream. And whoever is the best Indian will be the first to taste the ice cream when I get back!"

"Oh, let's play," shouted Lamb Chop excitedly. "I want to be— "

"Hold it, hold it," Charlie Horse interrupted. "We have to have a system."

"Then I want to be the system," Lamb Chop volunteered.

"Oh, that was a funny joke, ole Lamb Chop," Hush Puppy laughed.

"It was?" Lamb Chop asked. She didn't get it.

"No, Lamb Chop," Charlie Horse explained, "a system is a plan. We must plan how to be like Indians—for example, I'm going to be the Indian chief, so I have to make myself an Indian village."

"Who said you was gonna be the chief?" demanded Hush Puppy.

But Charlie Horse was too busy to answer. Out of pointed paper cups, he made Indian tents (called teepees) and trees, too. In the middle of the village, he put a tiny campfire. It wasn't really burning, but it looked as though it was. Near the campfire was a tiny totem pole with lots of funny faces piled on top of one another. Lamb Chop helped Charlie Horse make little eggshell Indians to live in his village.

While Charlie Horse worked away on the dining room table, Hush Puppy complained, "Just 'cause Charlie Horse says he's chief don't make it so. Ah got as much right as he do to be the Indian chief."

"No, you don't," called Charlie Horse, without looking up from his work. "I'm a better Indian chief because of my Indian pony."

"Where have you got a pony?" asked Lamb Chop.

"I haven't *got* a pony—I *am* a pony!" grinned Charlie Horse.

"That don't count," sulked Hush Puppy. "Ah don't care what you say. Ah want to be the *chief* Indian chief," he muttered, as he left the room.

Lamb Chop trailed him, saying, "—and *I* want to be—"

3

But Hush Puppy, still muttering, interrupted her. "What Ah need is a balloon."

"I don't want to be the balloon," cried Lamb Chop.

"Oh, that was another funny joke, ole Lamb Chop," Hush Puppy roared. "Ah meant that Ah need a balloon to make an Indian brave."

"Why would having a balloon make an Indian brave?" wondered Lamb Chop. "Having a balloon doesn't make *me* brave. It scares me, because I know it's bound to pop!"

"No, Lamb Choppie," explained Hush Puppy, "a brave is what they call a young Indian man. When Ah make myself some braves, Ah'll really be the Indian chief, 'cause then Ah'll be in *charge* of somebody. Ah think Ah can make an Indian brave out of a balloon."

And he did.

Baby had been awakened by all this activity, and now she was sitting in her playpen, just watching. Baby didn't want to be an Indian. She didn't even know what an Indian was. Baby talked a lot, but she didn't say real words. Not yet. She made funny noises which sounded like some foreign lan-

guage. The only time you could understand her was when she repeated what you had just said.

As Hush Puppy pasted colored bits of paper onto the balloon, to make it look like an Indian brave with war paint on his face, Lamb Chop turned to Baby.

"Nobody else wants to hear what I want to be, so I'll tell you. I want to be—"

But Baby interrupted Lamb Chop, too. "I wanna be—" Baby echoed, repeating what Lamb Chop had just said. Baby liked the way Lamb Chop's words felt in her mouth, so she said it again. And again. She chanted, "I wanna be— I wanna be—"

Lamb Chop sighed, "Poor Baby. You want to be an Indian, too, I'll bet, and you're stuck in that silly cage. I'll make you an Indian headdress so you won't feel left out."

Lamb Chop cut a feathered headdress out of an old road map, and she put it on Baby's head.

"There," said Lamb Chop.

"Dere," echoed Baby, and she wore it for at least thirty seconds. "Dere," Baby repeated, and she ripped it to shreds.

"Hush Puppy, come help me," called Lamb Chop.

"Anythin' Ah can do for you, honeychile, Ah'll do!" said Hush Puppy.

"Help me lift Baby out of her cage," said Lamb Chop.

"Except that. Ah cain't do that—Not right now."

"Why not now?" demanded Lamb Chop.

"Because Ah got mah hands full of puppet." And Hush Puppy showed Lamb Chop the second

Indian brave. It was a puppet, and he had made it out of an empty matchbox.

"That's really good, Hush Puppy," admired Lamb Chop. "What's your puppet's name?"

"Willy," answered Hush Puppy, "Willy B. Brave."

"Can I try your puppet?" asked Lamb Chop.

" 'Course, Lamb Choppie—any puppet of mine is a puppet of yours." And he took off the Indian puppet and gave it to Lamb Chop.

"Thank you," said Lamb Chop. "And by the way, now that your hands aren't full of puppet anymore, will you lift Baby out of her dumb cage, please, please?"

Hush Puppy stood staring at Lamb Chop. "You sure suckered me into that one, little lambie." And then he picked up the big Baby and put her down on the rug, so that she could crawl about. Hush Puppy took back his Indian brave puppet and admired it once again. "Oh, mah goodness, we really are movin' along in the Indian department."

"Yeah," called Charlie Horse, "by the time Shari comes back with the ice cream we will all be Indians."

"Oh, yes, yes," agreed Lamb Chop, "—and I will be—"

"But we better hurry," Charlie broke in. "Now, as chief, I am—"

"As chief, you am *nothin'*!" shouted Hush Puppy, and he punched Charlie Horse's arm.

Hush Puppy was the younger of the two boys. He knew that Shari would not let Charlie Horse hit him back, so Hush Puppy sometimes took advantage. Right now, Charlie Horse wanted to punch Hush Puppy, but he stopped himself. He just pushed the puppy, and down he fell.

Lamb Chop didn't like it when the boys fought. In the first place, they never fought with *her*, so she felt neglected. Besides, the fights generally ended with Hush Puppy in tears, and Lamb Chop *did* like Hush Puppy. A lot. So now she sat down on the floor, right next to Hush Puppy. He was trying to decide whether or not to cry, and Lamb Chop said, in her cheeriest voice, "Why don't you *both* be Indian chiefs—and then I will be—"

Charlie Horse scowled. "No. In the old days, the best Indian hunter became the chief. Let's see who's the best Indian hunter."

"No fair," complained Hush Puppy. "No fair—Ah never hunted for Indians before."

"No, Hush Puppy," Charlie Horse said, "Indian hunters means that the Indians do the hunting." Charlie Horse was glad that Hush Puppy had forgotten to cry, and he was anxious to change the subject. "C'mon, Hush Puppy," he shouted, "let's be Indian hunters." So they played Arrow in the Circle and Flying Feather and lots of other games.

Now Charlie Horse always criticized Hush Puppy when they played. Today he did, too.

"Gee, Hush Puppy," he teased, "your aim is no good at all."

Hush Puppy retorted, "Nothin' wrong with mah aim—Ah aim to beat you!" And Hush Puppy tried so hard that Charlie Horse even let him win one game.

"Phooey!" groaned Lamb Chop, sitting all alone. "Everybody said what he wanted to be except me, and I wanna be—"

"Hey, here comes Shari," Charlie Horse shouted, looking out the window. Everybody ran to meet her.

Shari put the ice cream down in the kitchen, and before she could take off her coat, Charlie Horse dragged her into the living room to see his Indian village. He told her that he was the chiefest Chief, and that Hush Puppy was the bravest Brave. And when Charlie Horse bragged that he was an Indian pony, Hush Puppy surprised them all! He had made an Indian hobbyhorse for himself, using an old sock and a little broom.

"And what about Lamb Chop? What were you, Lamb Chop?" Shari asked.

But Lamb Chop was not there. They looked in the dining room. They looked in the living room. They looked under things and in things and called, "Lamb Chop!"

Baby echoed, "Namtop!"

But there was no sign of the little lamb.

"Gee," said Charlie Horse, "she tried to tell us what she wanted to be, and nobody listened. Maybe she got mad and went outside."

Everybody was feeling very sorry for Lamb Chop when suddenly they heard her giggling. They all ran into the kitchen and there she was. Lamb Chop's face was painted brown—and green—and yellow—and red!

"Oh, Lamb Chop," gasped Hush Puppy, "that's good. You look like a real Indian. Is that war paint you got on?"

"No," smiled Lamb Chop, "it's ice cream. It's chocolate—and pistachio—and vanilla—and strawberry."

And they looked and saw that Lamb Chop had finished almost all the ice cream.

The only ice cream that Lamb Chop had *not* finished was a blob that had fallen to the floor beside the table. In the excitement, no one noticed it, except Baby. She not only noticed it, she stuck one fat little toe smack into the melting lump. It felt soft and squishy and cold and wet, and she liked it! She liked it so much that she put that entire fat, wet little toe into her mouth! Nobody noticed *that*, either. The others could only think of one thing—Lamb Chop had finished all the ice cream!

"I tried to tell you, but you wouldn't listen to me," Lamb Chop laughed.

"But you tried to tell us what you wanted to *be*," said Charlie.

"That's right," said Lamb Chop. "I wanted to be the first one to eat the ice cream!"

And everybody laughed, and then they all played Indians—except for Shari.

She had to go out and get some more ice cream.

PART 2

Indians As Far As the Eye Can See!

Charlie Horse built his Indian village right on the dining room table. Later, when dinner was ready, he had to take it all apart to make room for the food. Build *your* Indian village in a big box top (from a dress box or any gift box), and you won't have to wreck your settlement at mealtime.

If your box top is deep enough, you can even draw the rest of your village on the sides.

TEEPEES

Pointed paper cups make instant teepees. Or twist a sheet of paper into the shape of a cone, and tape it. Cut away the uneven edges at the bottom of the cone so that your teepee sits flat on the ground. Clip off the pointy end of the cone or cup to make a hole in the top of the tent. (Real Indian teepees always had open tops, because the Indians built fires inside their tent homes, and the smoke escaped through these high openings.) Break two cotton swab sticks in half, and glue the half sticks into the hole on top. The sticks will look like the tent poles holding up your teepee.

Paint or crayon any designs you wish on your teepee. (Stripes or dots, suns or moons or stars— please yourself and you'll please your eggshell Indians.) One small cut on the bottom of the teepee will make a good tent flap. Make the cut and then fold back the flap, or cut out a little upside-down V-section to make a permanent door. Remember, Indian settlements need lots of teepees.

TREES

Make trees out of pointed paper cups (or cones twisted out of sheets of paper), too. Cover the entire outside of a cup or cone with green paint or crayon. Stick the eraser end of a sharpened pencil into a gum drop, marshmallow, or bit of clay so that the pencil will stand upright. Place a green cup (tree-top) over a standing pencil (tree trunk). Make several trees and scatter them amongst your teepees.

CAMPFIRES

Break some cotton swab sticks or toothpicks in half, stick one end of each into red food color, place them so that they brace one another to form a teepee-shaped campfire, and glue in place.

EGGSHELL INDIANS

With a needle, poke a hole in each end of an egg. Then pick away at these holes until they are a little bigger than the head of a pin. If you blow gently into the hole at one end, the egg will plop out of the shell, through the hole at the other end. (If your egg cracks as you poke the holes, put a piece of cellophane tape over each end of the egg *before* you start.) Blow the insides of the egg into a bowl, and keep for next morning's omelet. Gently rub your empty egg with soap powder, and rinse thoroughly. This will help paint and glue stick to the shell.

To make your Indians, cut a two- or two-and-a-half-inch heart out of cardboard. Glue the egg to these cardboard "feet" so that it stands upright.

Cut a little blanket out of construction paper (just a strip long enough to reach around the egg, shaped like the body of a small boat).

Paint or crayon a design on the blanket, and glue it around the egg. Either paint little eyes peeking out from under the blanket, or cut them out of paper or colored tape, and glue them in place. Make a multicolored headdress of pieces of paper (about an inch tall), cut like feathers, glued to a strip of cellophane tape, and then stuck onto the Indian. You can make your Indian a chief with lots of feathers, or a brave, with just one.

Your eggshell Indian can be a puppet. Make him as described above, but do *not* give him any cardboard feet. Instead, enlarge the hole at the bottom of the egg until your pointer finger can fit in. Place one such Indian puppet on each hand, and let them walk along the back edge of a table (you hide under the table). If you push your boxtop Indian village right up to the edge of that table, it will look as though your Indians are walking along a back road, behind the teepees.

TOTEM POLES

The Indian settlements on the West Coast of America and Canada often had big totem poles which told the history of their tribes. Charlie Horse used empty matchboxes to make his totem pole. Small boxes or the cardboard tubes inside rolls of paper towels will do just as well.

Wrap each little box neatly with paper, and glue one on top of another (or cover your cardboard tube with horizontal two-inch strips of paper, each of a different color). From colored plastic tape or construction paper, cut out lots of eyes, noses, mouths and general shapes of all sorts—squares, skinny strips, triangles, circles. If you use plastic tape, stick pieces of tape onto wax paper *before* you cut the features, and then cut through both the paper and the plastic tape. When you are ready to assemble your totem pole faces, these plastic features will easily peel off the wax paper and will still stick to your covered boxes or cardboard tube. Features of construction paper should be pasted, glued, or rubber-cemented in place.

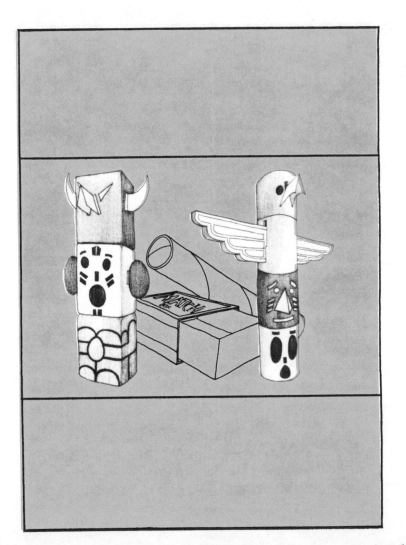

Work on one box or strip at a time. Make a face with ears that stick out on the sides, a nose that juts out in front. Make one box or strip into an animal or bird, the next into a weird and wonderful human face.

You can make this kind of totem pole with large boxes, too, for full-size cowboys-and-Indians play, or as a room decoration.

It's exciting to make a family totem beside a Christmas tree. Just have each member of your family decorate all his gift boxes Indian style, and then pile the faces, one on top of another, for "opening night"!

INDIAN PUPPETS

Hush Puppy took one of the empty match-boxes from Charlie Horse's totem pole and made himself an Indian puppet. (He called it Willy B. Brave, remember?) Here's how you can make yourself a matchless Indian brave:

Separate the two parts of a small empty matchbox and throw away the inside drawer. Cover this outer shell with construction paper or colored plastic tape. Cut a thin band of paper or tape, and attach a tiny feather to it. (If you don't have a real feather, a little paper feather will do.) Paste this headdress near the open top of the box. Now cut and paste eyes, a nose, a mouth, and two ears on the covered matchbox.

Making your puppet's body is as easy as 1-2-3—fingers, that is. Hold your hand with the last two little fingers folded onto your palm and the other three extended as in the picture. Now drape a handkerchief or paper napkin evenly over the extended fingers. Hook a rubber band over the handkerchief around finger number 1, pull it in back of your pointer finger (2), and hook it over the handkerchief and around your thumb (3). The head (your matchbox Indian) is slipped onto your pointer finger (2). The thumb and middle finger

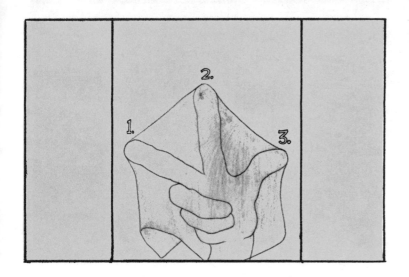

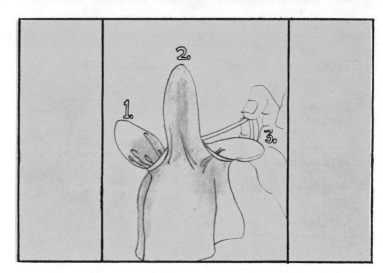

(1 and 3) become your new friend's hands—and there he is, right at your fingertips, ready to do your bidding. Don't forget to give Willy B. Brave a hatchet. Just paste a tiny paper blade onto a toothpick or cotton swab stick.

You can make Willy B. Brave out of an empty egg, too. Just follow these instructions, but instead of covering the face with paper or plastic tape, paint it, and then stick the features and headdress onto the eggshell. Complete your puppet by putting it onto the easy napkin puppet body described above.

For really happy hunting make yourself a Bouncing Brave out of a balloon, as Hush Puppy did. Cut features and feathers and feet and hands and hatchet out of construction paper. With dabs of rubber cement, paste the features and feathers onto the balloon.

17

Make "Catstairs" for arms and legs. Two Catstairs, with hands attached, get pasted on each side of the balloon, and another pair of Catstairs, with feet attached, go on the bottom.

Now Catstairs are accordion-folded strips of paper. (Nobody knows why they have that silly name, but it's what everyone calls them, so why shouldn't we?)

Glue or tape two long strips of paper together with their ends overlapping.

Place your finger firmly on top of the two connected ends. With the other hand, bring one of the loose ends (end A in the picture) over your finger and fold it down. Place your finger on top of the little center pile and (with the other hand, again) bring the loose end (end B, this time) over your finger and fold it down. Continue to do this until both strips are entirely folded. Paste or tape the ends together. Attach hands and feet to the end of the Catstairs and glue the hatchet to one hand. Tie a string around the knot on top of your Indian, and he'll do a jiggly war dance for you.

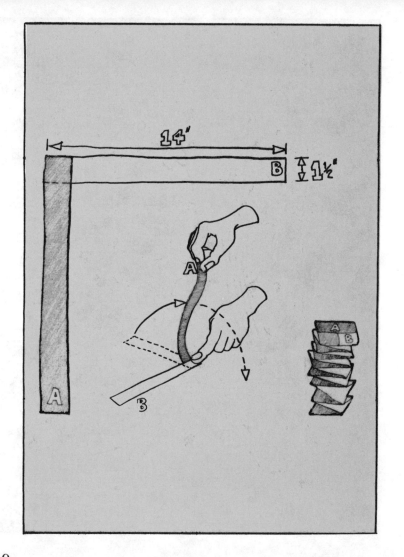

20

INDIAN HEADDRESSES

Lamb Chop made Baby an Indian headdress that was really a feather in her cap. You can make feather headdresses in many ways, depending on the materials that you have at home.

The perfect material for making a feather headdress is feathers. (Isn't that logical?) Very few homes have feathers floating around, but if your home is the exception, start with a strip of paper long enough to go around your head, plus a few inches to overlap when the ends fasten together (use a big safety pin). The feathers can be taped to the back of this strip.

If you do *not* have real bird feathers, you can cut and color big paper feathers, and make your headband exactly the same way.

Corrugated paper (that bumpy thick paper used to wrap breakable things) is fine for creating feather headdresses. Cut a long two-inch-wide strip of corrugated paper, and then stick the thin shaft of the feather into each "pocket" of the corrugated paper. Insert as many real or paper feathers as you have, wrap the headdress around your own head or your papoose's, and fasten it in back.

Road maps have colorful (and easy!) feather headdresses hidden in their folds! Most road maps come folded in half, and then accordion-pleated. Leave them the way they are when you get them, and cut as shown in the picture. When you open the pleating, you'll have a strip of double feathers attached to a band. Don't open the map entirely— leave it folded in half. Wrap the band (with feathers pointing up, please) around your forehead, pin it behind your head with a safety pin, and let the extra feathers cascade down your back.

For a newspaper headdress, open a double sheet of large (not tabloid-size) newspaper. First fold it in half along the already existing centerfold. Then, in the same direction, fold it in quarters, and, once again, in eighths. Open the sheet, and following the lines you have just made, accordion-pleat the sheet of newspaper. When it is completely accordion-pleated, you'll have a long, thin strip. Cut the same pattern outline suggested above for the road map headdress. Don't extend the point of the feathers up to the top of the paper; let them reach about halfway. When you open your accordion pleats, you'll have a band of paper with lots of

21

22

floppy feathers attached. You can fasten this newspaper headdress with a safety pin or tape.

INDIAN MASK

If the headdress doesn't make you feel like a real Indian, perhaps the Indian Bag Mask will!

Put a big clean paper bag over the head of whoever is to wear the mask. Carefully make two chalk or crayon marks on the part of the bag directly over the eyes. Draw a line on the bag running down the length of the nose, and place a dot on the spot that's over the center of the mouth. Take the bag off and cut out eyeholes, a nose flap, and tiny round mouth opening. With bright crayons or poster paint, color flashing eyes around the eyeholes, a vivid smiling—or snarling, if you prefer—mouth around the mouth opening, and typical war paint designs all over the face. Make two slits (about one inch apart) near the top of the bag and insert a feather into the top slit and out of the lower one. (A colorful paper feather will do just as well.) Draw large ears on the side of the bag, and cut along the outer rim of each ear, leaving the ears connected to the bag in the same way that *your* ears are connected to *your* head. Bend the ears forward, and then place the bag over your head.

For a surprising touch, insert through the mouth opening (and grasp between your lips) a party "blower"—one of those paper whistles that starts all rolled up, straightens out with a funny noise when you blow through it, and then snaps back.

INDIAN PONY (*The Sock Hobbyhorse*)

Hush Puppy made his Indian pony from a single sock that the laundry had been kind enough to return. He was putting his hobbyhorse together for a single afternoon of play, so he cut the ears and eyes out of paper and pasted them onto the sock. If your hobbyhorse is to be a gift, cut the features out of leftover bits of fabric and sew them in place. This little fellow can be made in about fifteen minutes, but he'll give somebody hours of pleasure "horsin' around"!

You will need:

A sock (the thicker, the better)

Clean ripped nylon stockings or other bits of material (for stuffing)

A broom (a toy broom or a household broom)

Bits of ribbon, heavy string or wool

Bits of paper or fabric

Glue, or needle and thread

Here's how: Stuff the sock very full of discarded nylons. Insert the broom handle deep into the stuffed sock (twisting and turning it to get it through the stuffing, well toward the heel of the sock). Tie the sock tightly around the broom handle with a piece of string or ribbon (see illustration). Cut round eyes, the size of quarters or half-dollars, depending on the size of the sock, and triangular ears, out of the paper or fabric. Glue or sew the eyes and ears in place. Cut and tie the ribbon, string or wool into eight to fifteen bows, and glue or sew

them in a row down the back of the horse's head. That's his mane! Wrap one piece of ribbon or string around the front of his face—as if you wanted to keep his mouth shut! Glue or sew it in position. Firmly attach the center of a much longer piece of ribbon or string to the place in front of his face, where his nose would be. Allow a long loop and then tie a knot. This is your hobbyhorse's reins. You've become Tonto, pronto. Hi-ho Silver, away!

INDIAN GAMES

Charlie Horse and Hush Puppy played the Flying Feather game. It's also fun for two *groups* of children. The players (or groups of players) stand at opposite ends of a table. A feather is set in the center of the table, and the contestants try to blow the feather off their opponent's end of the table. When the feather blows off one side, the player (or players) on the *other* side gets a point. When a contestant (or team) gets fifteen points, the game is over. A small piece of tissue paper, lightly crumpled, will substitute for the feather.

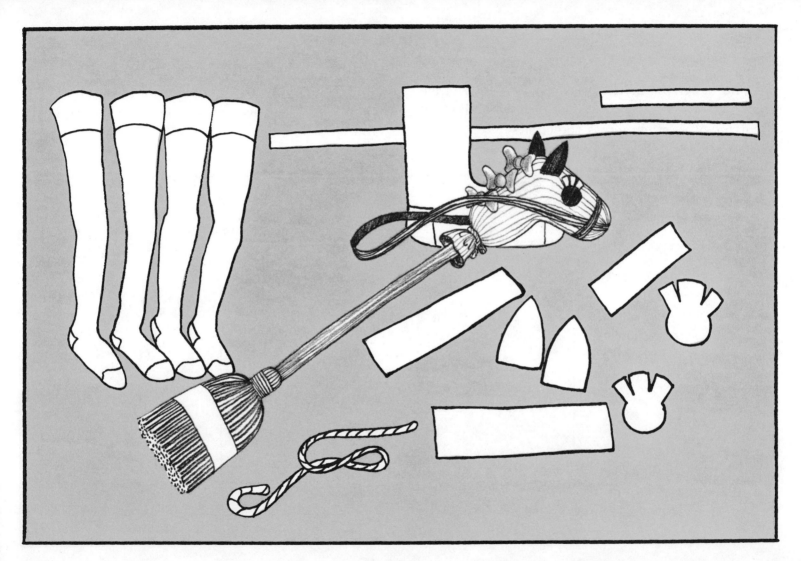

To test his aim, Charlie Horse (that well-known Indian hunter) challenged Hush Puppy to a game of Arrow in the Circle. He made a circle of his thumb and pointer finger and then he laid a cotton swab stick across the circle.

The aim of the game is this: Using only that one hand, toss the stick into the air, and as it comes down, make it go through the circle of your fingers. You can use a piece of a soda straw as an arrow, too!

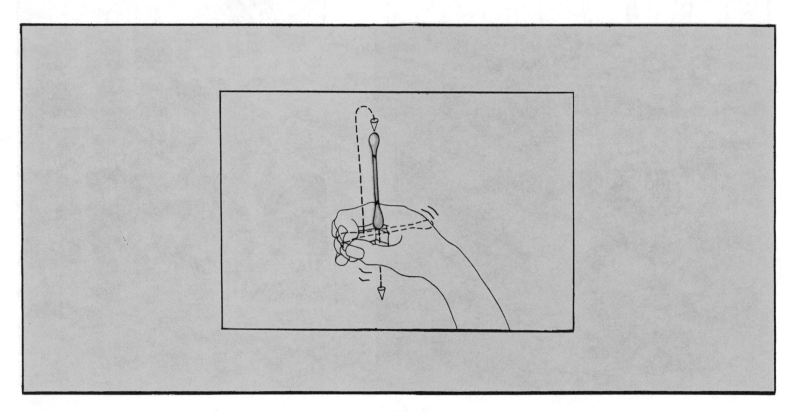

Lamb Chop's Green Thumb

PART 1

A Short, Moving Story

As the big orange van pulled away from the house, Shari held out the Teddy Bear.

"That's it, Lamb Chop," she said. "The moving men have packed everything but you, me and Teddy Bear. Shall we go?"

Lamb Chop sat down on the steps in front of the house. "Oh, I don't want to move to an apartment," she said. "The flowers you grow are so pretty here in the country."

Shari laughed, for they weren't *really* in the country. The house in which they had lived since before Lamb Chop was born was only a forty-five-minute drive from the city.

"How *do* you make all of these flowers grow?" Lamb Chop asked.

Shari said, "I have a green thumb. I'll bet you do, too!"

Lamb Chop looked down at her tiny hand. "No," she replied, "my thumb's red."

Shari smiled. "When people say you have a green thumb, it means that you have learned to be good at caring for growing things."

"Oh," said Lamb Chop, "then you *have* got a green thumb! You're good at caring for me, and I'm a growing thing."

Shari interrupted, "No, Lamb Chop. People with green thumbs grow pretty flowers and lovely lawns."

Lamb Chop looked at her thumb again, and said nothing. In fact, it wasn't until they were in the car, driving toward their new home, that Lamb Chop showed Shari her thumb.

"I guess I'm lucky it's *not* green," she said sadly. "Even if I could grow pretty flowers and a nice lawn, we'd never be able to fit them into our new apartment."

"Would you like to grow a big lawn?" asked Shari.

"Yes," sighed Lamb Chop, "but I'd need a house to go with it."

"Lamb Chop," said Shari, "I promise you that by the end of this week, you will have a house, and a lawn, right in the apartment."

"Will I be able to water the lawn, and cut it, too?" asked Lamb Chop.

Shari nodded her head, but would say no more.

The car stopped next to their big building, and they took the elevator to the apartment. Lamb Chop ran from room to room and in her excitement, forgot all about the garden and lawn. For the next few days Shari and Lamb Chop spent all their time opening cartons and deciding where to put things in their new home.

But at the end of the week Lamb Chop suddenly ran to Shari and said, "You promised that I could have a lawn in the apartment. Where are we going to put it?"

Shari thought for a minute and then she took some pens and pencils and paper clips out of an old cigar box. She stood the lid upright. Then, with tape, she attached two small sticks to the back of the box to keep the lid in this upright position.

She filled the box with earth from an old flower pot, sprinkled grass seed on the earth, and with a fork gently "raked" it through the dirt. Next Shari cut a piece of paper that was exactly the same size as the cigar box lid. On the paper she drew a pretty house with shutters, and flowers, too. After crayoning the shutters and flowers many bright colors, she pasted the picture to the inside of the cigar box lid.

Lamb Chop stood watching as Shari filled the watering can with water. "There," said Shari, handing the watering can to Lamb Chop, "you'd better water your lawn."

"What lawn?" asked Lamb Chop.

Shari giggled. "Why, the lawn in front of your house, of course." And Shari pointed to the picture on the cigar box lid.

As Lamb Chop sprinkled water on the earth in the box, she asked, "I can't really grow a lawn here, can I?"

"Lamb Chop," said Shari, "if you have a green thumb, you can."

The next morning, as Shari was pouring the orange juice, she reminded Lamb Chop to water her lawn. The morning after that, Lamb Chop got

her watering can without being told, and went to the cigar box. And what do you think she saw? Grass! Tiny bits of young grass all over the earth in front of the house.

"It's a lawn!" cried Lamb Chop.

"Not yet," said Shari. "Wait until tomorrow."

The next day the earth in front of the house in the picture was *covered* with short grass, and the day after that, the grass came up to the windows of the house. And by the end of the week, the grass was as high as the top of the door.

"Shari," begged Lamb Chop, "you promised that I could cut the grass in front of my house."

"I always keep my promise," said Shari. "Get your scissors."

Lamb Chop looked in her toy box. She searched through her drawers, and finally found her scissors in the box with her paper dolls. She brought the scissors to Shari, and together they cut the grass.

"Well," said Shari, "now you know a secret about yourself."

"What's that?" asked Lamb Chop.

"Lamb Chop," said Shari, "there's no question about it. You've got a green thumb."

PART 2

How Does Your Garden Grow?

If you don't have a cigar box, any cardboard box will do, as long as you line it carefully with a double layer of aluminum foil so the water won't soak through.

Instead of sticks you can use pencils or cotton swabs taped to the back of your box to keep the lid in an upright position.

Little white picket fences are simple to make out of cotton swab sticks or toothpicks, because they glue together easily in any position you wish.

You can really make your house a home by sticking trees and flowers right into the lawn. Cut out paper leaves and blossoms, and tape or glue them onto toothpicks and cotton swab sticks, bits of pencils or crayons, which will serve as stems and trunks. In the same way you can make tiny signs for your lawn—signs like "Beware of Dog" and, of course, "Keep Off the Grass."

Another good way to go to seed is to lay a waxed milk carton on its side and cut away the long side panel that is now on top. Fill the container with moist soil and add lima bean seeds for quick and pretty results.

Shari's mother is a schoolteacher, and she has always brightened her classroom and her own kitchen with lovely foliage and flowers, grown from kitchen cuttings. She suggests that you gather together these things:

Carrots, potatoes, sweet potatoes,
   radishes (any or all of them!)

Pebbles (if you want them)

Shallow plate of water

Toothpicks

Glass of water

Then remove the greenery plus the top inch of radishes or carrots, and place these tops on pebbles in a shallow plate of water, cut end down. Potatoes and sweet potatoes, which grow long and leafy vines, should be handled differently. Stick two toothpicks into the potato, one on each side near the middle. Half fill a glass with water and place the potato into the glass so that the toothpicks rest on the lip of the glass and keep the potato from sinking. (Potatoes don't swim, you know!) If about one-third of the potato is in the water, the plant will root.

I'll SEE ME IN MY DREAMS

PART 1

Click, Click

"Ohhhhh—don't *do* that, Hush Puppy," said Shari irritably, and Hush Puppy jumped! He was watching a scary old monster movie on TV, and hadn't even heard Shari come into his room.

"Don't do what, ole Shari?" answered Hush Puppy. "Ah didn't do nothin'."

"You did. You went---" and Shari took three little sniffs.

"Nothin' wrong with that, Shari," answered Hush Puppy. "That's called breathin'."

"No," said Shari, straightening Hush Puppy's blanket. "That's called sniffing, and you should be *blowing* that nose of yours instead."

Hush Puppy was sick in bed with a cold, but it wasn't really bothering *him*. It was bothering Shari. Hush Puppy was so interested in the old movie he was watching that he kept forgetting to blow his black little button of a nose.

"You stayed home from school to get well, not to watch television," said Shari, and using the remote control unit she flicked off the set—*click, click*. As she pulled down the window blinds Hush Puppy clicked the picture back on, pleading, "Ohhhh please, Shari, Ah gotta know if them beetle monsters find out where the spacemen are hiding up there on the moon—jes' let me watch 'til the next commercial—please?"

Shari continued to darken the room, and by the time all the curtains had been closed, the lights turned off, and the pillows fluffed, the next commercial had appeared. With a final *click, click,* Shari turned off the TV, and that was that!

Hush Puppy put his head down on the pillow, and in the midst of grumbling ". . . but Ah don't need a nap, ole Shari," he fell asleep.

But not fast asleep. Not sound asleep. Something was obviously disturbing Hush Puppy's

slumber. He tossed. He turned. He moaned. He groaned. Even in his sleep Hush Puppy knew that he was having a nightmare. But that didn't make him feel any better, because it was such a scary one.

In this frightening dream Hush Puppy was on the moon. He knew it was the moon because he had seen it before, but this time something was different. He blinked at the bright lights and vivid colors, and then he remembered. The last time Hush Puppy had seen the moon was on his black-and-white TV set. But now he wasn't *seeing* the monster movie—he was *in* it! Not as plain ole Hush Puppy, of course. He was "Buck" Puppy, the leader of the spacemen, driving his small flying saucer right over the scaly backs of the big moonbeetles.

Suddenly, in his dream Hush Puppy found himself riding like a cowboy, smack on the back of one of the big beetles. He galloped off to rescue his assistant (who looked something like Shari, only she had pointed ears and she was wearing a tight, shiny red space suit). Two simply enormous beetles were struggling with Shari, and then the largest one seized her and carried her away, screaming.

Hush Puppy didn't exactly hear her scream, because there were no sounds or noises in his dream. Not a word could be heard—but Shari certainly *looked* like she was yelling a lot, as this big beetle carried her off to the top of a mountain. There he ripped off his beetle costume, and guess who it was? The beetle turned out to be "Buck" Puppy in disguise, and he had saved her life!

Then the entire group of beetle monsters had "Buck" Puppy and Shari cornered in a cave. Hush Puppy didn't know how they had gotten there, but there they were! ("Ah must've slept through that part of mah dream," thought Hush Puppy. "Ah'm sorry ah missed it.") "Buck" Puppy tried to shoot the beetles, but his empty ray gun just went *click, click,* and since the beetles were getting closer, Hush Puppy did the only logical thing a puppy can do in this kind of situation—he screamed for help!

Hush Puppy, sound asleep, was still screaming when Shari ran into the room and turned on the lights. She had to shake Hush Puppy to wake him, and he tried to tell her about this nightmare, but his sobbing covered the words. Shari held him in her lap and comforted him, but Hush Puppy refused to go back to sleep.

"That was just a nightmare, Hush Puppy," said Shari. "There are no beetles. This isn't the moon. You see?" Shari pointed to her fuzzy bathrobe. "This isn't a shiny red space suit."

Hush Puppy buried his head in Shari's shoulder and continued to sob. "Please don't make me go back to sleep," he begged. "Mah bad dream will come again when it's dark."

"Well," said Shari, "let's put you in charge of the dark. I'll give you my flashlight to keep under your pillow. If it gets too dark, you can just flick on the light and you'll feel better—okay?"

Hush Puppy thought about it for a moment. "Well, Ah guess that's okay," he said.

Shari got up to fetch the flashlight, but Hush Puppy was still clinging to her hand, and she could see that he didn't want to be left all alone. She

pushed the button on the TV remote control box and *click, click* turned the set back on to keep him company, and to take his mind off his nightmare until she returned.

The moon monster movie was still going strong on TV. There were the beetles—there were the spacemen—in fact, everything was just as it had been in his nightmare, except there were no vivid colors—and there was no "Buck" Puppy in this old black-and-white movie.

Hush Puppy took one look and yelled for Shari. When she came racing back into the room, he excitedly said, "Watch me kill those bad monsters with mah ray gun—they'll never come into mah nightmares again." And aiming the TV remote control box, he *click-clicked* the movie off.

Then, with a flashlight under his pillow and a new sense of power, a contented Hush Puppy snuggled back to sleep.

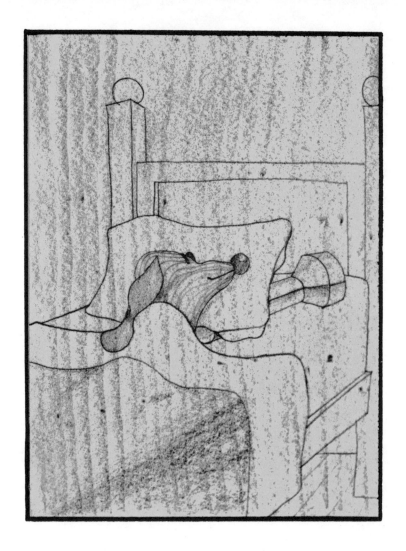

PART 2

Quick as a Flashlight

After an hour or so, Shari heard giggling and scuffling and shuffling, and jumping and bumping and thumping, and then more giggling from Hush Puppy's bedroom. She opened the door a crack and peeked in. It was dark, but Hush Puppy was holding the lighted flashlight so that it threw a circle of brightness onto the white wall.

Lamb Chop was standing about halfway between Hush Puppy and the wall, and she had her hands twisted in the oddest position. Her palms were facing her. Her thumbs were crossed and touching, and her little mitten hands were flapping. Shari looked at the wall and saw why. Lamb Chop was making the shadow of a bird, and it was flying.

Shari was so amused that she forgot to knock. She barged right into Hush Puppy's room, and as she walked toward Hush Puppy, Lamb Chop cried out in fright.

Shari stopped in her tracks. "What's the matter, Lamb Chop?" she asked quickly.

"Oh—" stammered Lamb Chop, "that's you."

"What's me?" said Shari. Then she realized that she was standing close to the flashlight, and her shadow on the wall was very tall.

"Shall I shrink a bit?" said Shari, walking slowly toward the wall. Her shadow got smaller and smaller as she got closer and closer to the wall. When she was standing right next to it, the shadow was just about her size.

"You can turn that little birdie you made into a big eagle, by moving your hands farther away from the wall," said Shari.

Lamb Chop put her thumbs together again and backed toward the flashlight. The bird got bigger and bigger, and soon it filled the circle of brightness on the wall.

"That's still not as scary as *your* shadow, when you walked in," laughed Lamb Chop.

Shari held up her hand. "You can turn your bird into something—well, if not scary, at least—creepy!" Shari made the shadow of the bird, and then suddenly separated her fingers and curved them a bit.

She wiggled all her fingers and moved both hands, still joined by the thumbs, slowly in one direction. The shadow looked just like a spider crawling across the wall.

Hush Puppy shouted, "Don't be afraid, ole Lamb Choppie—Ah'll save you from the spider." And he turned off his flashlight.

The spider was gone. So was the circle of light.

"Oh, please—let's do more," begged Lamb Chop. "You're not too tired, are you, Hush?"

"Turn on the flashlight, and you'll find somebody who will wake him up," promised Shari.

Hush Puppy was as curious as Lamb Chop to see what Shari was talking about. On went the light. Up went Shari's hands. She fumbled for a moment and then screeched, "There—look at that!" Shari had her hands together, with the fingers folded—but all it looked like was a handful of fingers. It wasn't until Shari opened and closed her thumbs and said, "Cock-a-doodle-doo," that they recognized the outline of the rooster.

Then Shari pointed her fingers *front*, instead of holding them up. She kept her palms together, and suddenly, they saw the shadow of a horse.

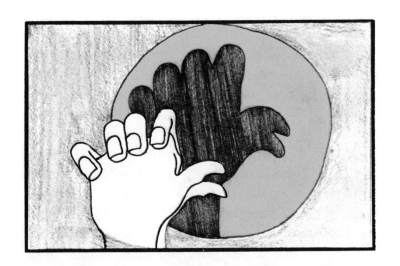

Hush Puppy made a horse, too. He moved his pinkie up and down, which made his horse's mouth move.

His horse said, "Hi y'all."

Lamb Chop giggled. "Your horse has a Southern accent, just like you do, Hush Puppy."

"My goodness, we're turning this place into a barn," called Shari. "Old MacDonald has nothing on us." Well, that's all she had to say.

"Old MacDonald had a farm—" sang Lamb Chop, moving her hands frantically, trying to shape another animal on the wall beside her.

"Ee-yai, Ee-yai-Ohhhhhooooo," howled Hush Puppy, in another key entirely.

"And on this farm he had a—a—duck!" continued Lamb Chop.

"A duck—a duck?" muttered Hush Puppy.

"You know—quack, quack?" And as she quacked, Lamb Chop opened and closed her fingers in time with the quacks, and she found her duck! Her other hand became the tail feathers. It was a ducky duck! Shari couldn't quite figure out how to do the duck shadow until Lamb Chop showed her.

"How'd you figure that out, lil' Lamb Choppie?" said Hush Puppy admiringly.

"Easy—she used her head," answered Shari. And trying to be silly, Shari used her head. She stuck her right arm up to her forehead, and then froze that way when Lamb Chop yelled, "Hold it—don't move, Shari. Hush, come hold the flashlight—hurry!" She carefully placed the big flashlight in Hush Puppy's hands. Then Lamb Chop went to Shari's side and lifted Shari's left hand until the fingers stuck out past the back of her head.

Shari kept twisting her head to see what her shadow was creating on the wall, but every time she shifted her position, Lamb Chop groaned, "Don't look—just take my word for it—it's a swan. You used your head and made a swan. Hush Puppy, can you see it? Here—" Lamb Chop pointed to the top of Shari's head "—this is the swan's curved back."

Hush Puppy was all smiles. "Tomorrow morning, when Ah get back to school, Ah can show all mah class how to make all these animal shadows, right, Shari?"

"Wrong, Hush Puppy," said Shari, flicking off the flashlight.

Lamb Chop reached the wall switch first, and the overhead lights came on. Hush Puppy's smiles were gone. "Which part of what Ah said was wrong, Shari?"

"Tomorrow morning," said Shari, still blinking from the bright lights, "you won't be in school—you have to stay home at least one more day to make sure that your cold is gone."

"Oh," whined Hush Puppy, "everybody else will be at school. I'll have nobody to play with."

Shari grinned. "Here." She handed him the big flashlight. "They have school, but you can have Old MacDonald's farm right at your fingertips, as quick as a flashlight!"

I SEE ME IN MY DREAMS

PART 3

To Catch a Shadow

When Hush Puppy finally returned to his classroom, he was a very happy puppy. His teacher's name was Miss Albert, and she was his friend. Not his best friend, because she didn't join in the pushing and shoving and racing and chasing in the school playground. She couldn't seem to catch a ball, and when she threw one, it was hard for *you* to catch it, because it always landed someplace else. But it was nice to talk to Miss Albert. She had good ideas, and she laughed a lot, and she made *you* laugh, too.

So when Hush Puppy stood up and told the class about the hand shadows he had made on his bedroom wall, she said, "Would you like to catch your shadow and keep it, Hush Puppy?"

Hush Puppy shook his head so hard that his long ears flapped as he spoke. "Cain't do that, Miss Albert. Soon as you flick off the flashlight, your shadow is gone for good."

Miss Albert smiled as though she had a secret. She sent Hush Puppy to the cabinet for the small slide projector with which they usually made pictures appear on the classroom wall. She asked Barry (who was bigger) to set up the tall easel, and she clipped a large sheet of black construction paper to the easel and put it about seven feet from the projector. Then Miss Albert set Hush Puppy on a chair, right between the easel and the projector. She asked him to turn toward the window so that she could see his face from the side.

Meanwhile, Jessica pulled down the shade. The projector threw a small strong beam of light across the darkened room. Miss Albert moved Hush Puppy's chair forward and then back a bit 'til she found the position which made Hush Puppy's shad-

ow just the right size on the easel. The outlines of his face were quite clear.

"Oh, you have a nice silhouette," said Miss Albert.

She took a sharpened pencil from Valerie's desk. Then, standing close to the black construction paper (but not in the beam of the light), she traced the outline of Hush Puppy's shadow.

Hush Puppy didn't dare peek as he posed, but he was pleased. Miss Albert said he had a nice silhouette, and he didn't even know he had one!

"There!" said Miss Albert with relief. "You can get up and move around, Hush Puppy. I've caught your silhouette."

Hush Puppy was distressed. If he had a nice silhouette, he didn't want her to catch it. He wanted to keep it. He timidly walked over to Miss Albert, who was standing near the window.

"Excuse me, m'am, if— "

"Just a minute, Hush Puppy. I have to be very careful with your nose and mouth." Miss Albert was cutting the black paper along the pencil lines that she had drawn. "I'm so glad to have this bright daylight in which to work—Turn off the projector, please, Lisa."

Hush Puppy reluctantly helped Lisa put the machine away and returned to his seat as Miss Albert went to the easel. She had the black paper in her hand, and when she pasted it on top of the white paper on the easel, Hush Puppy saw what Miss Albert had done. She really had captured his shadow!

"There's your silhouette, Hush Puppy— caught once and for all!" smiled Miss Albert.

Hush Puppy smiled, too. He *did* have a nice silhouette. He could see that now, and although Miss Albert had caught it, he knew she'd give it back to him.

"I'll bet Shari'll frame this for you, Hush Puppy," said Miss Albert.

And Shari did.

Whether you want to catch your shadow (and make a silhouette) or just play with it (and make hand-shadow animals), here are some things for you to remember:

. . . The closer you are to the wall, the sharper and smaller the shadow will be.

. . . Your light should come from only *one* strong source or bulb. More than one causes fuzzy outlines.

. . . Make sure that all other lights are out, and all curtains, shades and drapes are drawn so that there are no "light leaks."

. . . Jewelry (on ears, neck or hands) confuses the outline of your silhouette or shadow.

. . . As you make hand shadows, try not to watch your hands. Look right at the shadows that you are creating on the wall, and make any changes to improve the appearance of the shadow animals without looking down at your fingers.

PART 1

Diddle Diddle Dumpling, Little Lamb

Lamb Chop had a Grandma Ann,
And, as grandmas often can,
Grandma Ann knew how to knit,
And what she knit, really fit.

Grandma Ann made her a sweater.
Lamb Chop liked that sweater better
Than anything she'd ever had.
Now you might say, "That's not bad."

51

Well, summer days in mid-July
Are often hot and always dry.
But one thing now was hot and *wet*,
And that was Shari's sweatered pet.

Lamb Chop said she wouldn't take her
Sweater off—you couldn't make her.
Out she went to play in it,
Although it was a heavy knit.

Shari, watching her, repeated,
"Dear, you're getting overheated."
"No," said Lamb Chop, though she felt
That in a moment she might melt.

Now tag's a racing chasing game,
And hide-and-seek is quite the same.
But Lamb Chop was a nut for pink,
So on *this* day, she didn't think!

Behind a bush she tried to hide,
But though the bush was thick and wide,
Charlie found her in a wink
'Cause through the leaves, he saw that pink!

Charlie sneaked around and tagged her.
As she ran, the branches snagged her,
Caught her sleeve and ripped her cuff.
Shari said, "Lamb Chop, enough!
Your sweater's really much too pretty
To let it get all knitty-gritty."

Lamb Chop looked. The sleeve was ripped.
The buttons down the front were chipped.
The bottom was unraveling badly.
Lamb Chop turned to Shari, sadly.

"Do you think that Grandma Ann
Will fix it? Oh, I hope she can!"
And she began to cry. "Be still,"
Said Shari. "If she can, she will."

They went home, but had to wait
To make the call 'til it was late.
Grandma was a music teacher
So they knew they couldn't reach her
'til her working day was done
Then Lamb Chop dialed. That was fun.
"Grandma," said she, "you should see
The sweater that you made for me.

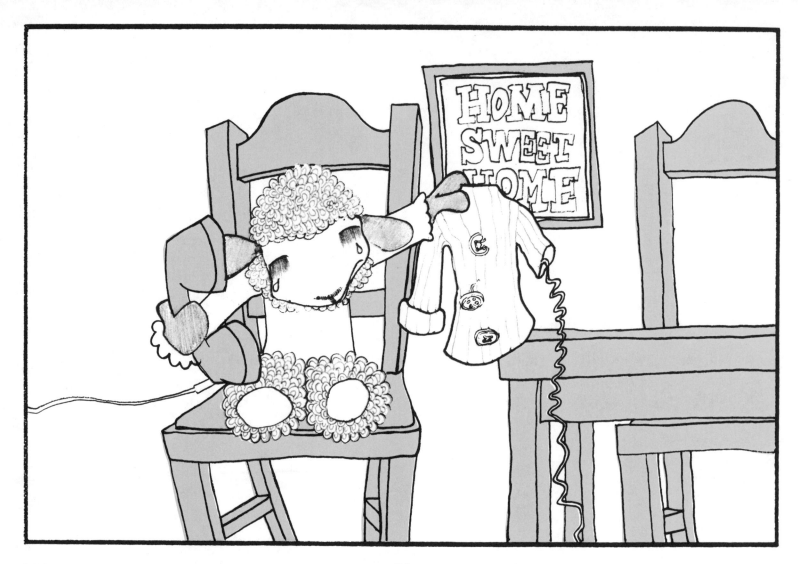

54

"It's a mess. The sleeve is ripped.
The buttons down the front are chipped.
The bottom is unraveling badly.
Can you fix it?" she asked sadly.

"Sure, I'll fix it," Grandma said.
"Get yourself prepared for bed.
I'll come soon. Now I suggest
You hurry up and get undressed!"

Lamb Chop got undressed and then
She put her sweater on again.
First her nightie, then her sweater.
"There," she said, "I feel much better."

Grandma came but couldn't get her
To take off that ragged sweater.
"Lamb Chop, how can I repair it,"
Grandma asked her, "while you wear it?"

"Fix it on me, 'cause I'm cold,"
Grandma Ann was finally told.
"Fix it on me, or I'll freeze.
Fix it on me won't you please?"

Lamb Chop hugged it 'round her tight.
"Grandma shouldn't have to fight
To fix your sweater," Shari said.
Lamb Chop simply shook her head.

"It's my favorite shade of pink.
It looks nice on me, I think,
Even though the sleeve is ripped,
And buttons down the front are chipped."

Grandma looked. The sleeve was ripped.
She took her scissors, and she clipped
A loop of wool, and pulled the strand.
The sleeve unraveled near the hand.

Lamb Chop looked. It broke her heart.
Her sleeve was coming all apart.
Grandma pulled the stitches out.
Wool was lying all about.

Lamb Chop was about to cry.
Shari said, "I wish you'd try
To understand that Grandma's right."
Lamb Chop started to recite:

"Diddle Diddle Dumpling, my son John,
One shoe off and one shoe on.
I am just like that boy John—
One sleeve here, and one sleeve gone."

"Diddle Diddle Dumpling?" Grandma smiled.
"You are such a funny child.
Please don't cry. I couldn't bear it.
I will hurry and repair it.

"In the meanwhile, here's some wool."
Grandma gave a final pull,
And cut off what had been the sleeve.
Grandma then got up to leave.

Lamb Chop's lap was really full.
It held a heap of crinkled wool.
"Grandma," she said, "I believe,
"You'll need this wool to fix the sleeve."

Grandma said, "I have some more
Of that pink yarn. It's in my drawer.
Keep that heap of wool, don't lose it.
Someday you might want to use it."

Lamb Chop shrugged, "No, I can't knit.
I've tried. I can't do it a bit."
Shari laughed, "It's difficult.
It's even hard for an adult.
But I know something you *can* do.
Tomorrow I'll teach it to you."

"Goodnight, mother," Shari said.
And then she put her lamb to bed.
Lamb Chop woke up once to say,
"If knitting's hard, can I crochet?"

Shari tucked her back in bed.
"Dear, I promise," Shari said,
"We'll make something that I think
Will look just lovely in that pink."

Next day, in the park they found
Two big twigs right on the ground.
And with the yarn from Lamb Chop's sleeve,
Shari taught Lamb Chop to weave.

The sticks were crossed. The yarn was wound
Across each stick, and then around.

There was really nothing to it.
Lamb Chop found that she *could* do it.

The design was very pleasant.
"Grandma's gonna get a present,"
Lamb Chop said, "'cause I believe
That if you give, you should receive."

So, when Grandma Ann walked in
Lamb Chop chanted, with a grin,
"Diddle Diddle Dumpling, Grandma Ann,
You always do the best you can.
You made my sweater good as new,
And now I've got a gift for you."

Grandma Ann was tickled pink.
She said to Lamb Chop, with a wink,
"I'm really glad your sweater fits.
And thank you for my present, it's
The nicest gift I'll ever get.
Are you happy now, my pet,
My Diddle Diddle Dumpling, little lamb?"

Lamb Chop laughed and said, "I am."

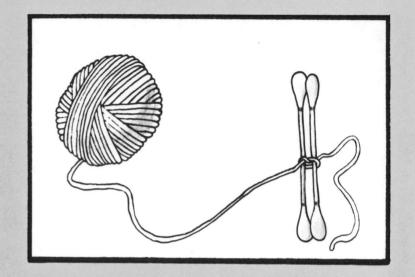

PART 2

How To Weave a God's Eye

Shari taught Lamb Chop how to weave something called "God's Eyes." Shari knew how to do it because she's a Girl Scout Leader, and Girl Scouts make these woven patterns out of twigs and branches they find on their hikes.

God's Eyes (which look like big eyes) were made up a long, long time ago by the very first Indian tribes that lived in America. They would hang these Eyes of God on the walls of their caves or place them in their children's hair. The Indians felt that nothing bad could happen to them if the Eye of God was always there—watching over them.

God's Eyes are very, very easy to make, once you get the rhythm of the weaving.

Use twigs, pencils, cotton swab sticks or any kind of thin rods. Unroll about two feet of your ball of wool, and lay it straight out on a table. Lay your two sticks next to each other across the wool, and tie a single knot around the middle of both. Pull it very tight, and then tie another knot on top of the first.

Twist the sticks so that they cross one another and form a giant cross. Pinching the center of the cross between your thumb and pointer finger, wind

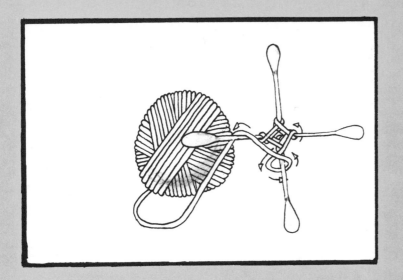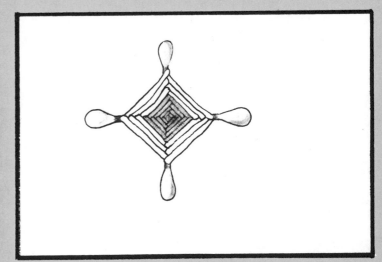

both strands of wool (the one connected to the ball, and the short left-over end) around one stick (right next to the knot, where the sticks cross). Then stretch your double strand over to the next stick to the right.

Shift the position of your thumb and pointer finger so that you can easily wrap the strand over, under, and around this next stick on your cross. Now stretch the strand across to the third stick, always moving in the same direction (it's a good idea to keep winding the wool clockwise). As you wind the yarn around the sticks, keep adjusting

your hold on the cross of sticks so that the stick around which you are wrapping is always nearest you, pointing in your general direction.

Soon you will have used up the short end of the yarn, and will only be wrapping a single strand around the sticks. Keep winding in this way until your design is the right size.

To change colors in the middle of your design, stick the strand you're working with securely between stitches in the back. Then insert the beginning of the next color of wool under some other stitches in the back—and continue winding in the same way. You might like to let the knobby ends of the twigs, or the little white cotton puffs of the swabs, extend past your design, or you may prefer

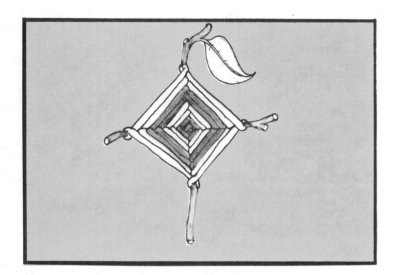

to wind right to the ends with the wool. When you've gone as far as you wish, cut your yarn and wedge the loose end between some of the stitches in the back of your design.

If you want your wool wound right to the very end, dab each of the four stick-ends with a glue that dries clear and transparent, or with a blob of shellac.

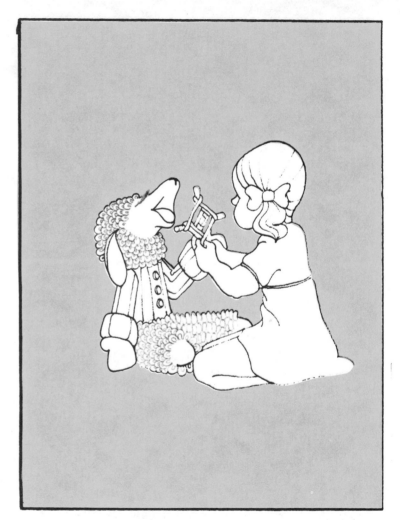

PART 1

The Disappearing Act

Hush Puppy loved to play with Steven. In the first place, Steven was nine, and so much more grown-up. He had two bigger brothers of his own, and since Steven sometimes needed to be older than somebody, Hush Puppy had become his "little buddy." Every couple of days Steven would walk home from school with Hush Puppy, and stop in for a cookie or a pretzel before continuing up the block and across the street to his own house.

This particular afternoon, Charlie Horse wanted to play with Steven, too, which upset Hush Puppy so much that he shouted, "Go find your own friends!" Then Hush Puppy tapped Steven on the arm, called, "Race you to the front door!" and he

and Steven tore out of the room, leaving their glasses of milk on the kitchen table.

Charlie Horse felt left out, and he decided to attract some attention. He got an old rain hat from the hall closet, a deck of playing cards from his bed table, and then he ran through the apartment yelling, "Magic Show in two minutes—don't miss Charlie Horse, the Great Magician, doing his tricks right in the kitchen!"

Shari stuck her head out of her study. "Magician?" she asked.

"That's right," bragged Charlie Horse.

"As far as I know," muttered Shari, as she followed Charlie Horse through the hall, "five minutes ago you didn't know a *thing* about magic."

"That's right," repeated Charlie Horse.

"And now you're a great magician?"

"How's that for a trick?" laughed Charlie Horse, and he turned to face his audience, as they straggled into the kitchen to see what all the noise was about.

Lamb Chop begged, "Charlie Horse, can you do real magician tricks like making a rabbit come out of a hat?"

Charlie Horse swaggered to the table. "I'll do better than that—I am now going to make a rabbit disappear." Charlie Horse waved a fork over the hat, and then proudly picked it up, and showed the hat to be empty.

"Isn't that amazing?" he screamed. "Isn't that thrilling? The rabbit is gone—it's gone!"

Lamb Chop looked at the hat, then at Charlie Horse, and then she stared at Shari. Shari tried not to laugh, but Steven grinned at her, and she grinned back.

Lamb Chop complained, "Oh, no—there *wasn't* any rabbit in the hat to start with."

"Yes," said Charlie Horse quickly. "Yes, definitely. I made a rabbit disappear alright! You didn't see it because it was an *invisible* rabbit that I made disappear!"

Lamb Chop turned her back on Charlie Horse and walked out of the kitchen, muttering, "For *that* I missed the first part of my best TV show! Boy, I must be dumber than I look."

Hush Puppy picked up the glass of milk that he had left on the kitchen table and started to leave, too, but Charlie Horse excitedly snatched the milk from his hand, spilling some on the floor.

"I," announced Charlie Horse, "will now make this entire glass of milk miraculously vanish right before your very eyes."

Hush Puppy had turned to get some paper towels to wipe up the spill, but at this announcement he hurried to Charlie Horse's side, in order not to miss the miracle.

"You have to help me with this trick," Charlie said.

Hush Puppy shook his head. "No way, Charlie Horse. Ah cain't do no magic."

Very softly Shari corrected Hush Puppy's English. "You can't do *any* magic, Hush Puppy."

Hush Puppy looked sadly at Shari. "Ah know Ah cain't, Shari. You don't have to rub it in in front of mah friend."

Before Shari could continue, Charlie Horse, who felt that he was losing the attention of his audience, began to wave his arms frantically. "Okay, okay—all Steven and you have to do is say the magic word, and I will do the trick."

Steven and Hush Puppy stood close together, ready to help.

"The magic word is Mooooo—just like a cow—Moooo," said Charlie Horse.

Steven and Hush Puppy took deep breaths, and as loudly as they could they both said, "Mooooooo."

And as they did, Charlie Horse put the glass of milk to his lips and drank every bit of it.

"Ta Daaaa!" he shouted, with a white milk mustache on his upper lip.

"Oh," said Hush Puppy disappointedly, "Ah could have done the trick *that* way, too."

To which Charlie Horse replied, "Yes, but *I* did it, and let me tell you, it was delicious!"

Hush Puppy disgustedly took Steven's hand and started to stamp out of the room, but Steven patiently turned back to Charlie Horse.

"Okay, one more chance, Charlie Horse. No kidding now, do you know any *real* tricks?"

Charlie Horse picked up the deck of cards. "Every magician does card tricks, right?"

"Right—but do you?" smiled Steven.

Charlie Horse did not answer. With one swift fancy move, he spread the cards out on the table-

top, facedown, so that none of the pictures showed.

"Pick a card—any card, and don't show it to me," he said in a very magician-like way.

Steven started to pick a card, but Hush Puppy urged, "No, not that there one. That's the one Charlie Horse wants to force you to take. Ah know him. Take this li'l ole card down here—the one that's almost hidden."

Steven picked the card near the bottom of the deck, showed it to Hush Puppy, and held it close to his chest so that Charlie Horse couldn't see it.

Charlie Horse now said, "Alright, sir, would you quietly say the name of your card into my ear."

Steven looked at the card once again. It had a picture of a lady on it, and black patterns that looked like three-leafed clovers.

Hush Puppy whispered, "What *is* that lady's name?"

"She's the Queen of Clubs," Steven said so softly that Hush Puppy asked, "What?"

"No—no," Charlie Horse interrupted impatiently, "whisper the card's name into my ear." Steven did so.

Charlie Horse then stood very straight and shouted, "Ladies and gentlemen, Steven's card is the Queen of Clubs."

Steven snapped, "That's no trick. I *told* you what my card was!"

"Of course, how *else* was I supposed to know?" demanded Charlie Horse, and then he took a deep, silly bow.

By the time he straightened up, Steven and Hush Puppy had left. Shari handed him a paper towel and wordlessly pointed to the milk he had spilled on the floor.

Charlie Horse protested, "That's *it*? That's *it*? You're not even going to tell me what you thought of my big trick?"

"What big trick? None of them worked!" said Shari.

"I mean the *disappearing* trick," said Charlie Horse.

Shari was bewildered. "What did you make disappear?"

Charlie Horse smiled, and he gestured to the empty room. "The audience—I made my whole audience disappear."

66

"Congratulations, I think," laughed Shari, and she went to the phone. "Now please make that milk on the floor disappear, too!"

Charlie watched Shari dialing. "Who're you calling?" he asked.

But at that moment Shari delightedly said, "Hello, Poppa. Oh, I'm so glad you're home!"

Charlie Horse was glad, too. Shari's father, called "Doc" by all of his friends, was a good magician—a *real* magician who could make money seem to drop out of your nose, and who could hold a rope and make knots tie and untie themselves, just like—well, just like magic!

"Poppa, Charlie just did a magic show for us, and he—" Shari listened for a minute as her father said something. "Oh, no, Dad, his magic was just awful." Charlie made a face at Shari, and she quickly continued, "But he's very funny. If you could teach Charlie Horse some tricks that really *work*, I think he'd love it!"

Charlie Horse was nodding his head so hard that his hat fell off.

Shari continued, "Oh, lovely—come soon, and stay for dinner—fine. Bye, Daddy." She hung up the phone.

"How soon is *soon*?" asked Charlie eagerly.

"By the time you've done your homework, my Dad will be here."

And so he was. Charlie Horse took Doc off to his room and locked the door.

They didn't even come out when Shari announced that all the food was on the table, and finally Hush Puppy angrily pounded on Charlie's locked door and loudly demanded that they come to dinner.

After the dishes were done, Charlie Horse put on his second magic show of the day.

First he made a rabbit appear—not a real live rabbit, but a picture of a rabbit. Next Charlie Horse made a glass of water disappear. Last of all, he did some funny tricks with sticks. It really was a good magic show. Everybody said so.

PART 2

Tricky Stuff!

You can put on a good magic show, too. Here's how Doc and Charlie Horse prepared the tricks:

THE MAGIC RABBIT

To make the picture of the rabbit appear, Doc found a stiffish piece of paper in Charlie's room

before the show. (They used a brown manila envelope. You can use part of a regular white envelope, a somewhat heavy sheet of stationery, or the back of an old greeting card.) Charlie Horse cut it into a rectangle six inches tall and two and a half inches wide.

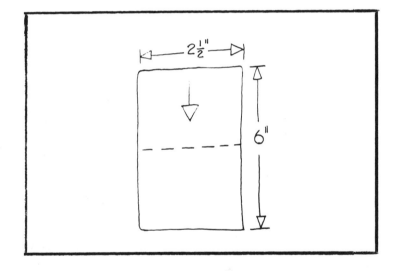

Then they folded it in half, measured down three-quarters of an inch from the fold, and lightly marked a few dots at this spot. They measured three-quarters of an inch up from the bottom edge, and made a few dots there, too. They measured *in* a half inch from each side, marked the spots, and then Doc drew a square U, following their faint markings.

Doc carefully cut along the lines of this square U so that it became a flap. Now Charlie Horse held the bottom edges of the paper together with one hand, and gently lifted this flap with his other hand, trying hard not to fold or crease the top of the flap as he carefully bent it back. Doc traced the sides and the *top* of the opening onto the bottom part of the paper, drawing an *upside-down* square U. Then he opened the folded paper, and cut out this flap, too.

On the lower flap (which was the upside-down square U) Charlie Horse drew the outline of a high hat. On the top flap he drew the same high hat, but with a rabbit popping out of it. He made sure that the hats were both about the same size, and both resting near the bottom of their flaps. (You can trace Charlie's high hat and rabbit, or draw your own.)

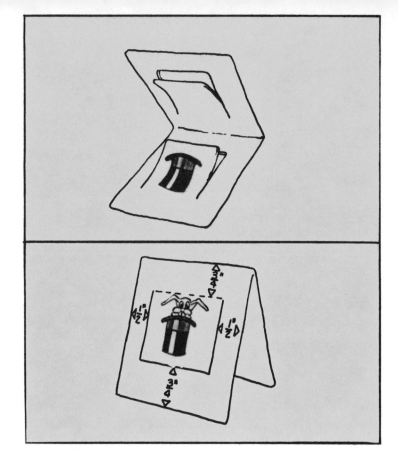

Doc showed Charlie how to slip the bottom flap (with *just* the high hat on it) through the top slit, so that it came in front of the top flap. When they pulled the bottom flap, with the empty high hat, *over* the flap which had the rabbit and the hat drawn on it, it looked something like this:

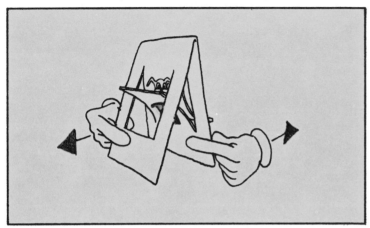

When Charlie Horse did his magic show, he held the folded paper so that the hat was facing the audience. In his left hand he gripped the front part of the folded paper, while his right hand held the back part.

He showed his friends the picture of the empty high hat, and as he said the magic words "Rabbit, appear!" he pulled his right hand back and left hand forward, sharply. In other words, he pulled the flaps apart with a quick movement, and immediately put them back together again. As he did, the flap with the empty hat on it slid out of sight,

and now, amazingly enough, a rabbit seemed to have popped into the high hat!

Everybody begged Charlie Horse to do the trick again, but Doc said, "No, no—a magician never does a trick more than once."

"DRY" WATER!

For his second trick, Charlie Horse made a glass of water vanish. He used three paper cups for his water trick, and you should, too. In his room Charlie secretly prepared one of the cups by carefully cutting out the flat bottom of the cup.

Then he stuck the three cups into one another, with the bottomless one (Cup B) in the middle.

When he did the disappearing water trick for his audience, first Charlie Horse poured water from a pitcher into the top cup (Cup A). (*See Fig. 1.*)

He lifted Cup A and placed it on the table. (*See Fig. 2.*) Then he asked his audience to tell him which cup contained the water. They pointed to Cup A, and he agreed. He said, "Now, I want you to try and keep your eye on where the water goes!"

He picked up Cup A and poured the water into Cup B (which didn't have the bottom). (*See Fig. 3.*) Then he put Cup A aside.

Next he carefully lifted Cup B and put it down on the table, on the other side of Cup C. (*See Fig. 4.*) Everybody thought that Cup B had the water in it, but because he had secretly removed the bottom of Cup B, the water had gone right through into Cup C.

Now Charlie Horse asked Lamb Chop to tell him where the water was. Lamb Chop (and every-

body else) excitedly pointed to Cup B.

"Oh, no—oh, no—you weren't watching!" said Charlie Horse happily—and he picked up Cup B (holding it so that his hand covered the hole in the bottom), and he turned Cup B upside down.

Then he put the bottomless cup carefully on the table, picked up Cup C and poured the water from *it* into Cup A. The water had vanished from Cup B, and somehow had traveled into Cup C.

Charlie Horse casually piled the cups into one

another, nesting them as before (with the bottomless cup in the middle and the filled cup on top), and he said, "A real magician never does a trick more than once—but I'm not a real magician, so I'm going to do *this* trick twice!"

Twice was enough. Charlie horse crumpled up the cups and threw them away before his audience got a chance to examine them. Then he moved on to his last miracle.

TRICK WITH STICKS

"This is a stunt with sticks," he said, dropping a handful of cotton swabs on the table. (When *you* try these stunts on *your* friends, you can use toothpicks, cotton swabs, or even pencils if you have enough of them.)

Charlie Horse handed Lamb Chop five sticks and said, "Can you make two triangles, using these five sticks, without bending or breaking them?"

Lamb Chop looked at the sticks. "I'm sure I could, if I knew what a triangle was."

Doc, Shari and Charlie Horse all started to speak at the same time. "A triangle is a—" They laughed, and stopped for a moment, and then all three began to talk to Lamb Chop once again.

Lamb Chop put her hands over her ears. "I can't understand when I get it from three sides," complained Lamb Chop.

Doc exclaimed, "That's like a triangle—*it* has three sides, too."

Lamb Chop leaned shyly against Shari. "*What* has three sides, too?"

Shari took four cotton swabs and made a square on the table. "What's this shape called?" she asked.

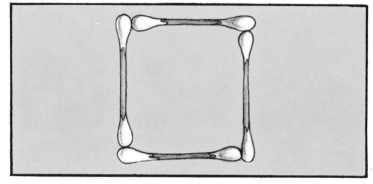

"A square," said Lamb Chop.

"Right—a square is a shape that has four sides," said Shari, "while a triangle is a shape that has only *three* sides." And then she made a triangle out of the cotton swabs, like this:

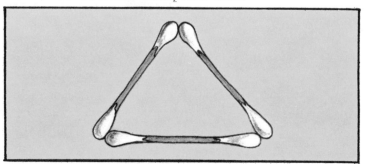

Hush Puppy picked up the two other cotton swabs and asked Charlie Horse, "You said the trick is to make two triangles, using only five sticks?" And before Charlie Horse could say yes, Hush Puppy added his two cotton swabs below Shari's triangle, so that the bottom line of her triangle became the top line of his, and it looked like this:

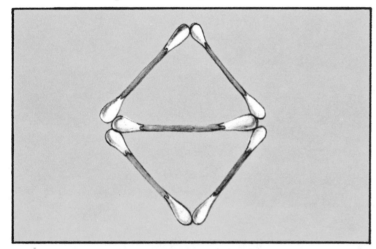

"That's really clever of you, Hush Puppy," said Doc. "You've got a sharp eye."

Hush Puppy was delighted. Charlie Horse wasn't so delighted. He seized the five cotton swabs and said, "Okay, smarty, there's five sticks, and here's four more. How many is that?"

"Errr—five and four?" muttered Hush Puppy. "Give me time—Ah'll get it—five and four—don't tell me—Ah got enough fingers to figure that one out—" And by that time, he had! "Nine," Hush Puppy shouted. "Five and four is nine!"

Hush Puppy was the smilingest dog you've ever seen, but his smile disappeared when Charlie Horse said, "Well, I can show you how five and four can make ten!"

Shari protested, "Oh, c'mon, Charlie Horse, that's—"

But she stopped protesting to watch, for Charlie Horse was hard at work. He laid out four cotton swabs as he counted, "One, two, three, four."

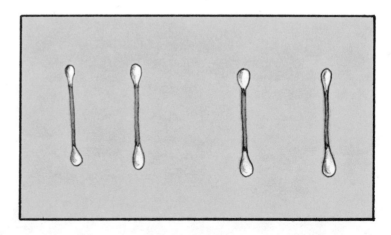

Then he took the other five, and added them to the four in such a way that they did, indeed, make ten—like this:

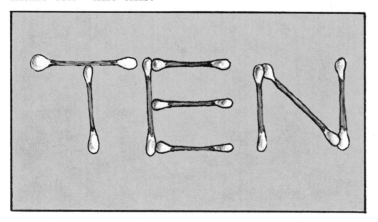

Shari stood up, tapped on the table and said to the youngsters, "Okay—okay—now it's my turn. Please help me show my daddy what a good magician *I* am." She turned to her father and announced, "When I say this magic word, Lamb Chop, Hush Puppy and Charlie Horse are going to disappear! The magic word is—*Bedtime*!"

And at that, all three scurried out of the kitchen, and off to bed, and the show was over!

Strictly for the birds

PART 1

A Bird in Hand . . .

"Oh, Lamb Chop, please stop whining! Nobody can tell that you're wearing a snowsuit under your costume," said Shari, as she zipped up the red jacket and then slipped the long black dress over Lamb Chop's head.

"Nobody can tell?" echoed Lamb Chop disbelievingly. "All bundled up like this, I'm the fattest witch in the neighborhood!"

Shari bent her head slightly, so Lamb Chop wouldn't see her smile, and fastened the black cape around the little lamb's neck.

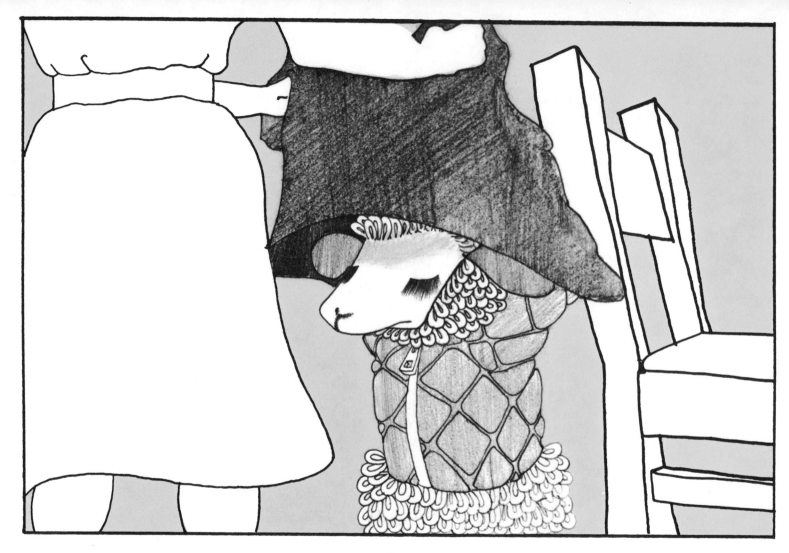

Lamb Chop squirmed out of Shari's grasp and protested, "A witch this overweight definitely couldn't fly around on a broom. She'd need a—" Lamb Chop suddenly stopped, because she saw the look on Shari's face. No longer smiling, Shari got up and walked to the sofa. She sat silently for a minute, and then beckoned for Lamb Chop to sit beside her.

"Darling," said Shari firmly, "it's freezing out—I don't ever remember so much snow at Halloween. Either put on your gloves and let's go, or we'll have to forget the trick-or-treating entirely this year."

"Is Charlie Horse going to have to wear his coat, too?" pouted Lamb Chop.

"Of course," said Shari. "It'll be freezing when he and the other big boys go out after dinner."

The cold air rushed in as Lamb Chop opened the door. Shari hurriedly buttoned her own coat, and out they went.

In the early evening light they could see a small pirate and a ghost trudging through the snow near the house next door. Lamb Chop called out, "Hello, Shawn," and the pirate lifted his black mask and peered in her direction. "I'm Lamb Chop, you silly," she shouted with delight, and the pirate muttered, "Oh, yeah," and turned back to the neighbor's front door as it opened.

Shari and Lamb Chop decided to begin their trick-or-treating at the top of the block, but as they started up the hill, Lamb Chop gave a small cry of distress and ducked under a low tree. She quickly reappeared, cradling the body of a tiny dead bird in her red mittens.

"What happened to it?" whispered Lamb Chop.

"I guess these little chickadees can't find food when the snow is on the ground," said Shari, and she took the bird from Lamb Chop, whose eyes were filling with tears. Shari knelt down near the tree and started digging in the shallow snow. "C'mon, help me. We'll bury the poor thing. That's really all we can do."

Lamb Chop bent down, too, but she was too busy thinking to dig. "We could go to all these houses, and then give our trick-or-treat candies to the birds, so that they wouldn't die." Lamb Chop scrambled to her feet, anxious to be on her way.

"Hold it, honey." Shari put the bird into the hole and covered it with snow. "Birds can't eat candy."

"Why not?" asked Lamb Chop. "Will they get cavities in their teeth?"

Shari brushed the snow off her knees as she rose. "Birds don't *have* teeth—just tongues."

Lamb Chop replied, "Then they could *lick* the candy."

Shari put her arm around Lamb Chop. "Sweetheart, when we get home from trick-or-treating, I'll show you the trick of making treats for the winter birds."

Lamb Chop stared down at the mound of snow under the bush and shivered. "I'm cold—let's go home."

Before dinner, Shari sliced the fat off the meat and cut it into chunks. Using a needle and a length of strong thread, she made a long string of lumps of fat. "Chickadees'll like this," she said to herself.

As Charlie horse cleared the table, he took the left-over scraps of bread from each plate, and crumbled them together into a paper cup. "Starlings'll like this," he said to himself.

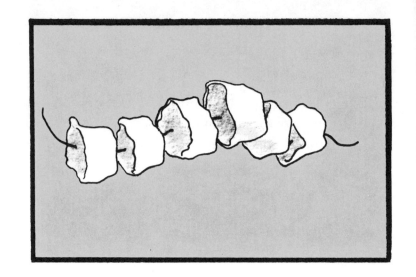

Shari cut an orange in half, and using a curved grapefruit knife, scooped out the juicy orange meat from each half of the shell. "Lamb Chop'll like this," said Lamb Chop to herself, and she took a big bite.

"Okay," laughed Shari, "that half is for you, but the rest is for the birds."

At Shari's request, Hush Puppy filled one half of the orange shell with peanut butter and the other half with pieces of orange meat and raisins.

Then he and Charlie Horse bundled up and raced off to do a bit of trick-or-treating before bedtime.

"What would you like for lunch tomorrow, Lamb Chop?" asked Shari.

Lamb Chop moaned, "When I'm all full, I hate to think about eating."

"Salmon or tuna?" said Shari briskly. "You decide, or I'll decide for you."

"Tuna," shrugged Lamb Chop.

So Shari opened a can of tuna, dumped the fish into a dish, and put it into the refrigerator. Then she washed the can and set it aside. They boiled a cup of sugar and a cup of water together for five minutes, then added a cup of left-over bacon grease. Lamb Chop stirred in cornmeal and bread crumbs until the mixture was firm, and they packed it into the empty tuna can.

"There," said Shari. In the morning we'll open our outdoor cafeteria."

The next day was crisp and clear and very cold. The top layer of snow had formed a crust of ice, and Shari and Lamb Chop left a trail of footprints as they took the birds' breakfast around to the yard behind their house. Shari was carrying the big

Baby, so Lamb Chop draped the string of chunks of fat over a low bush, and then hung the orange shells on the lowest branches of a tree. (Shari had threaded loops of string right through the orange skin.)

Lamb Chop wedged the tuna tin, full of the food mixture, securely into an elbow of the tree, between the trunk and one of the lower branches.

As they returned to the house, Lamb Chop played a game. She walked right behind Shari. She

only stepped into Shari's big footprints, and so she made no tracks of her own.

Later that day they returned with two little paper cups full of water. They left them under the tree, because the water that the birds usually drink was either covered by snow or had hardened into ice.

They found that the string of fat had been shaken off the bush, but there were no birds in sight. This time, as they walked home, Shari and Lamb Chop left no footprints at all, for the increasing cold had turned all the snow into ice.

The following day there were still no bird customers at their outdoor cafeteria. The food hadn't been touched.

Lamb Chop was bewildered. "Are you sure that birds like all that fat, Shari? I know *I* don't!"

Shari assured Lamb Chop that the birds needed to eat fat because their bodies were like tiny machines that used the fat as fuel, the way a car uses gasoline, and the birds turned the fat into heat.

"Can we bring something tastier tomorrow?" persisted Lamb Chop.

So, when tomorrow came, they brought apple slices. Lamb Chop was able to hang the slices on the low branches because Shari had pushed the ends of a wire hairpin into each slice.

But still no birds appeared. And although they went each day, and sprinkled nuts and seed in the melting snow, there were never any birds to be seen.

The snow was gone by the last day of the week, and the muddy ground was covered with puddles. Lamb Chop was quite wet when she and Shari returned from their walk. Shari put the little lamb's coat near the heat to dry, and went upstairs to take off her own soggy clothing.

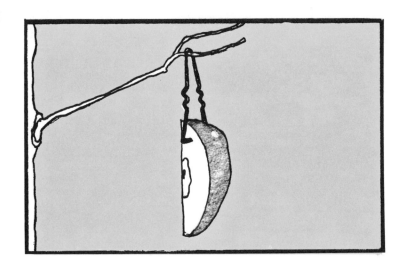

"Shari," called Lamb Chop, "are you making that funny smell?"

Shari came to the top of the stairs, took one deep sniff, and ran down the steps. "What on earth—!" She stopped suddenly at the base of the stairs, and then walked slowly, sniffing all the way, following her nose like a hound dog. When she reached Lamb Chop's coat, which was lying near the heat, Shari made a sour face.

"*You're* making that funny smell, Lamb Chop," she said. Shari picked up the damp coat and examined the lining. Then she poked around in the sleeves, and finally Shari put her hand into one of Lamb Chop's pockets.

"Oh," cried Shari, and when she pulled her fingers out of the pocket, they were covered with goo and smelled just awful. "Lamb Chop, what have you been keeping in this pocket?"

Lamb Chop looked down at the floor. Then she looked up at the ceiling, and it wasn't until Shari put the open pocket right under Lamb Chop's nose that Lamb Chop answered, "Well, every day I've been taking some of my dinner meat and stuffing it into my pocket. When you weren't looking, I put it under the bush for the birds. It just wasn't fair for me to eat all the meat, and only give them the fatty part. I wanted to give the birds some of the good stuff, too."

"I *thought* your appetite had improved," said Shari, and she dropped Lamb Chop's ski jacket into the sink.

"I guess birds just don't like your cooking," said Lamb Chop.

Shari filled the sink with warm sudsy water. "You're right," she laughed. "You've been leaving the best cuts of meat for our fine-feathered friends, and we still don't seem to have been able to attract a crowd. I must complain to my butcher."

Suddenly Shari wiped her hands dry, and walked swiftly toward the front closet. "C'mon, honey," she called over her shoulder. Lamb Chop scurried after her, and Shari helped Lamb Chop into her "going-out" coat, because her everyday ski jacket was soaking in the sink. "There," said Shari, "you're going to be the best dressed spy in town."

"Spy? Why, spy?" muttered Lamb Chop, but Shari just took Lamb Chop's hand.

Shari whispered, "Not a word, now!" to Lamb Chop as they entered the yard and huddled behind the hedge.

"Are we finally going to see birds eating our food?" Lamb Chop asked.

"No," said Shari. "And there's the reason why!" Shari pointed to the bush where they had been leaving the fat and seeds, and nuts and fruits—and the pieces of Lamb Chop's dinner meat. The neighbor's two large cats were slowly approaching. They rummaged under the bush, found what they were looking for, ate it and left.

"That was last night's hamburger, Lamb Chop!" complained Shari.

"Well, you gave me such a big one, and I did eat half of it," answered Lamb Chop.

Another cat sprang from the low branches of the tree (knocking off the food-filled orange shells), sniffed under the bush for a moment, and wandered away.

"No wonder the birds are staying away—your meat has attracted all the neighborhood cats, and cats eat birds, you know."

Lamb Chop looked surprised. "I didn't know that."

"Well," said Shari, "every *bird* knows that, and the poor little things are afraid that if they come to our cafeteria, they'll end up being *dinners,* instead of diners!"

Shari stood up, walked to the bush, and removed all the food. Then she reached as high as she could and hung it on the very ends of tree branches that were so thin the cats couldn't climb on them.

"There! The cats will have trouble reaching those—and the only food we'll scatter on the

ground will be nuts and seeds and other things that cats definitely don't eat."

"No more meat!" agreed Lamb Chop. "From now on, our outdoor cafeteria will be strictly for the birds!"

PART 2

The Trick of Making Treats for Birds

Make a foodshelf on your windowsill so you won't have to go out in bad weather to feed the little birds. Use a cookie tin, disposable aluminum dish from a frozen food package, or an old kitchen tray. Make sure it has an edging, so the seeds won't blow away. Fasten this tray to your windowsill, and serve any of the foods that Shari and Lamb Chop served to *their* feathered friends.

An excellent toy and feeding tray can be made of an old compact with a mirror in it. Clean out the powder compartment and fill the bottom with seeds. Fasten to the branches of a tree by tying a pipe cleaner or a piece of string securely around the hinge. Birds love to look in mirrors, and now your feathered friend can enjoy looking and talking to himself as he dines.

Cut down the sides of a small paper cup so that the paper cup is shallow. Thread a needle, stick it through both sides of the cup, make a loop and tie a knot. Mix a teaspoonful of peanut butter with an equal amount of crumbs and put this into your little paper bucket, and you can hang it right on the branch of a tree.

Birds also like hard-boiled eggs, crackers, popcorn, pumpkin seeds and bits of cheese.

PART 1

I Gave My Loves a Ribbon . . .

The last shreds of the Thanksgiving turkey were still showing up in lunch boxes when Shari began to hear it. "How many days 'til Christmas?" asked Lamb Chop.

"Oh, yeaaah, ole Shari," drawled Hush Puppy, "how many days *is* there 'til Christmas?"

Shari corrected him, "*are*—how many days *are* there!" And, ignoring the question, she hurried about her work. But that didn't make the question go away.

Even Baby babbled from her crib, "How many—Tismas?"

The question hopped around in the air for a few days, until one morning Shari said, "Well, tomorrow is the first of December. Christmas Eve is the twenty-fourth. How many days do *you* think there are 'til Christmas?"

Hush Puppy looked casually up at the ceiling, and whistled a few choruses of "Jingle Bells" so Shari wouldn't notice how hard he was figuring. Finally, he turned to her and shouted, "Twenty-four days, right?"

Shari said, "Right," and turned to leave the room.

But Lamb Chop pulled at her skirt. "How long *is* twenty-four days?"

Shari was stumped. She really didn't know how to answer. "Twenty-four days is twenty-four days long—I guess. What do you mean, how long?"

Now Baby got in on the fun. "Honong?" she asked insistently.

Shari grinned and started rummaging in the drawer that contained the gift wrapping materials. Finally she found what she was looking for. It was a roll of red ribbon. In Lamb Chop's bedroom, Shari tied the loose end of the ribbon to one of the poles holding up the bookshelves. Then, walking backward along the wall, she unrolled the ribbon until she had reached the foot of Lamb Chop's bed. There she tied the other end of the ribbon to the bedpost. The long ribbon ran along the wall.

"Is twenty-four days as long as that ribbon?" asked Lamb Chop.

"No, darling," Shari laughed, "but I'm going to leave you twenty-five secret messages on that ribbon. You may open one every morning, and when you've opened the last one, it will be Christmas morning."

Then Shari went to her desk, took out a small pad, and she wrote and wrote and wrote. Sometimes she seemed to be drawing a squiggly little picture on the piece of paper. Sometimes she just scribbled a few sentences. She folded each sheet of paper in half, and then tucked it into its own tiny envelope. On the back of each envelope she wrote a number, starting with "1" and ending with "25."

Charlie Horse, who kept trying to peek over Shari's shoulder, saw her write "25" on the back of the last envelope, and he yelled, "But you said there were *twenty-four* days 'til Christmas."

" 'Til Christmas," Shari said. "But December twenty-fifth is Christmas Day. Each one of these envelopes contains a Christmas activity or game or craft that you will enjoy doing. Number 25 will tell you what you can do on Christmas Day as well."

Shari hooked the flap of each envelope over the ribbon, so that the ribbon lay in the crease that connected the flap to the rest of the envelope. She then moistened the glue on the flap and fastened the envelope closed. Soon all the envelopes hung from the ribbon, with their numbers facing into the room.

Early the next morning Lamb Chop won the argument about who was to open the first envelope. ("The rule," she said, "is ladies first!")

The youngsters were busy 'til noon, following the instructions in the first envelope. They made lots of Christmas decorations for the front hall.

The next day Charlie Horse opened envelope Number 2. ("After all," he reminded them, "I'm the oldest!") And they spent a happy hour playing a game called "Packing Santa's Sack."

Lamb Chop, Charlie Horse and Hush Puppy argued over who would open envelope Number 3.

(Hush Puppy reminded them, "After all, dog is man's best friend. That means," he said angrily as he snatched the envelope, "that I'm the friendliest!") And they made fat and funny marshmallow snowmen and trees.

Then they let Baby open one, too, but she couldn't read it. Of course, she tried to eat it—and as they snatched the wet paper from her chubby fingers, the youngsters all shouted, "No, you're not supposed to *eat* this!"

Charlie Horse looked at the crumpled sheet and laughed, "Oh yes, we are!" For the instructions on Number 4 told them how to make delicious Christmas candy. They didn't have to cook this candy, so they made it all by themselves—and they ate it all by themselves, too!

For the rest of the month Shari didn't hear it once. No "How-many-days-'til-Christmas?" She didn't even hear any "What-shall-we-do-now?"s or "I-haven't-got-anything-to-play-with"s. She hardly heard the TV set, because all the youngsters had better things to do. Each afternoon they raced home from school. Sometimes they even brought a friend. They all scurried into Lamb Chop's room, and by the time dinner was ready, they had made

or done something that was fun.

As the days went by, Lamb Chop commented that her room was shrinking. It certainly seemed smaller as it began to fill up with Christmas decorations and the many gifts and packages they had wrapped, pasted, sewn, tied, painted, twisted, cut, dyed—Oh! What a jumble!

Whenever Shari suggested that they put away the paints, paste, scissors, brushes or bits of paper with which they were working, they would protest, all speaking at once, "We'll need them again tomorrow," "Mine isn't dry yet," "It'll get all squished."

The only neat spot in the room was the length of red ribbon. Each day another envelope disappeared, and before they knew it, it was Christmas Eve.

Only one envelope remained on the ribbon, hanging near the foot of Lamb Chop's bed.

"Oh, it looks so lonely," said Lamb Chop. "I'll bet Number 25 doesn't like being the only one on the line." Lamb Chop didn't like to think of *anything* being "the only one." She even felt bad about the single sock she sometimes found in her sock drawer. "What do you say—let's open the envelope?" she suggested, since nobody else had suggested it.

The others turned to see Shari's reaction. They had understood the "one-a-day" rule of this ribbon game, and all month long had been careful to stick to it. Now they expected Shari to say no to Lamb Chop's proposal.

But Shari just shrugged, "As you wish."

The youngsters all headed for the last envelope, and stopped only when Shari called, "Hold it—the rule is, if you open the envelope, you have to promise to do the activity described in it— right?"

"Right," they echoed, and since they all reached envelope Number 25 at the same time, they agreed that Lamb Chop would *open* it, and Charlie Horse and Hush Puppy would each get to read half of the message inside.

Hush Puppy read, "Merry Christmas—I hope you have enjoyed each of these ways to count the days 'til Christmas—" He turned to Shari, "Oh, yeaaah, Shari, you sure done it good—it was—"

But Charlie Horse couldn't wait. "C'mon, c'mon," he said brusquely, and he snatched the paper from Hush Puppy's hands, "my turn to be the reader." And he read, "Your activity for this last day is—" His smile disappeared, and he looked up at Shari.

Now *she* was grinning. "Read on, reader."

Charlie slowly continued reading, "—activity for this last day is to clean up all the mess you've collected over the past twenty-four!"

"Oh," groaned Lamb Chop, "do we *have* to do it tonight? That'll ruin our Christmas Eve."

Shari interrupted, laughing, "No, of course you don't have to do it tonight, honey." She started to take down the ribbon. "Tomorrow we'll clean up together. It won't take long if we all dig in—and then Lamb Chop will have a clean room to play in during these next ten days."

"Why ten days?" asked Lamb Chop.

"Honeychile," drawled Hush Puppy, "our Christmas vacation is ten beautiful days long."

Lamb Chop turned. "Shari," she said, "put that red ribbon back up! You have to figure out what we're going to *do* for the next ten days."

Shari continued to roll up the red ribbon. She said firmly, "For the next ten days, my friends, we are going to turn to the Table of Contents." She pointed to Lamb Chop's copy of *The Tell It—Make It Book.*

"Turn to the what?" asked Lamb Chop. "Which table is that? The one in the dining room?"

"The Table of Contents," said Charlie smugly, "is part of a book—that's what it is." And he walked toward the door, but not fast enough.

"Bet you don't know *what* part!" called Lamb Chop.

"Well, neither do you," snapped Charlie Horse.

Shari spoke quickly. Christmas Eve was no time to let them fight it out. "A Table of Contents is a list of everything in a book. It tells where to find things that you're looking for, and tomorrow we're going to turn to the Table of Contents and find lots of other activities in this book that will be fun to do at Christmastime."

And after *you* have tried the twenty-four ways to play at Christmas—which are listed in Part 2 of "How-Many-Days-'til-Christmas?"—see the page called "Hidden Christmas Treasures." It will give you enough Christmas-y things to do to keep you busy 'til *next* Christmas!

PART 2

Getting There Is Half the Fun!

If you want to play "How-Many-Days-'til-Christmas?" write each of these twenty-four games, crafts or activities on a separate piece of paper, tuck into tiny envelopes, and hang on a ribbon. You can put them in any order you wish. Perhaps you would prefer to simply hang one envelope for each of the nine or ten days of the Christmas vacation. Just pick the activities you like best.

Some of Shari's suggestions were art projects, for amusing gift wrappings or "I-made-it-myself" gifts:

1. Use popcorn, rice, puffed cold cereals, toothpicks, cotton, cotton swab sticks, or macaroni to create unusual pictures to give as gifts, or to decorate the tops of gift boxes. For a gift wrapping, start with a largish box, covered with solid-colored paper (even brown wrapping paper).

To make a gift picture, paint the *inside* of the lid of a big box, or line it with black or colored paper, or a scrap of fabric.

On a sheet of white paper draw just the outline of a design—something easy, like a snowman, a Christmas tree, or a simplified reindeer. Cut out this outline and trace it onto the surface of the lining in your box lid, or onto your wrapped package. From here on, you're on your own.

For example, if you have drawn the outline of a fat snowman, you could cover the entire inside of your snowman with rubber cement or glue, and fill it with popped popcorn! (Pre-popped popcorn that you buy is difficult to glue because it has oil on it. If you're popping your own, don't add butter or salt.)

After your snowman is all puffed out (that is, filled in) with popcorn, you can glue features or other details to the background, or to the popcorn itself. (Try using a line of unpopped kernels of corn for making the broomstick that the snowman is holding, and little toothpicks or straws taken off a real broom, to create the bristles of the snowman's broom. Glue on a bit of black paper or fabric for a hat, a little strip of material for a scarf, buttons or raisins for eyes, etc.)

Or draw the outline of a Christmas tree and fill it in with rice (which can be dyed with food coloring, dried, and then glued in place), or with macaroni (any size, any shape—spiral, tube, shell, elbow, straight, thin noodle). Macaroni also dyes well and glues nicely—particularly with rubber cement. Toothpicks, cotton swab sticks, even buttons, make fine Christmas trees. You might like to glue colored gumdrops (as Christmas balls) or paper stars to your tree.

Cotton swabs (with their white tips and sticks) will create a snowy tree. These also make excellent

beards for Santa Claus faces.

Try toothpicks, cotton swabs or bits of soft cotton to fill in your simplified outline of a reindeer.

2. On the top of a wrapped gift box use gummed silver stars to spell out the name or initials of the person to whom the gift is being given.

3. Wrap a box in solid-colored paper and glue on alphabet soup letters to form holiday greetings.

4. Put a decorative little tree on the gift box that is going to end up under the big tree. Form the little tree out of notebook reinforcements (gummed paper rings). Make the trunk three rings wide, four rings high. Then make the lower branches of the tree eight or nine rings wide, and build up your tree so that each branch has two rings less than the branch below. The very top of the tree (a single ring) should be crowned with a gummed star.

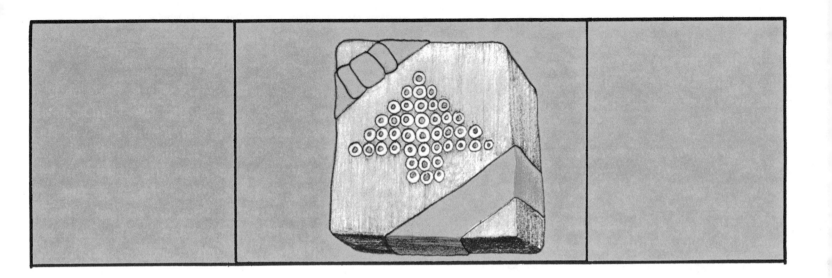

5. Draw a picture of a design or greeting on a piece of folded construction paper or on top of a wrapped gift box. Now go over what you have drawn with rubber cement (either use the rubber cement brush or a cotton swab stick). Sprinkle soap flakes all over the sticky surface, shake off the excess, and your design or greeting will be covered or outlined in "snow."

6. Write a greeting or party invitation on a piece of folded construction or typing paper. Write

very lightly, and then go over what you have done in red nail polish. Before it dries, sprinkle the polish heavily with salt. The frosty result has an interesting texture. This is attractive on top of a wrapped gift, too, to decorate the box or to name the lucky person who is getting it.

7. Cheap brown wrapping paper can be made into festive and lovely gift wrap by dipping sponges, wads of newspaper or scouring pads into poster

paints or finger paints, and pressing them here and there all over the paper, to create a textured effect. Handprints (the flat open hand pressed first into finger paint, then here and there on the paper any which way) also make *very* charming and personal gift wrap paper.

Other envelopes contained Shari's instructions for making Christmas decorations for 'round-the-house:

8. Before the big Christmas tree arrives, make your own. A delightfully gay balloon tree can be formed on the wall by attaching red or green round balloons with tiny bits of cellophane tape (use double-faced tape or roll a little circle of regular tape, sticky side out). Use a single balloon at the top, three in the next row, five in the next, etc. Two or three long balloons, placed up and down, will form the trunk.

9. Create a silver wreath around a wire hanger. Have the hook cut off, and pull the rest into a circle. Pad the circle with aluminum foil, pressing and pinching the foil into place. Then tape wrapped candy, lollipops or artificial flowers around the wreath, and top with a huge bow.

10. Make large No-Sew Socks to hang on the fireplace or to give as gifts. Cut two big identical sock shapes out of felt. (Pinking shears add to the effect.) Brush a border of rubber cement around one of the shapes, but not along the top edge. Press the other sock shape on top of the sticky one, so that they match exactly. Then cement felt cutouts (snowmen, stars, bells, trees) and sequins, rickrack, buttons, glitter on the front of the sock, and hang. On Christmas Eve, stuff with small goodies!

A few of the envelopes told how to decorate the Christmas tree in ways that were as much fun to do as they were to look at, when completed:

11. Cover your tree with "snow" that won't melt, won't burn. Use a rotary beater or electric mixer to beat two cups of packaged soap or detergent flakes or granules with about one-half cup of water. Add more soap or water, as necessary, until

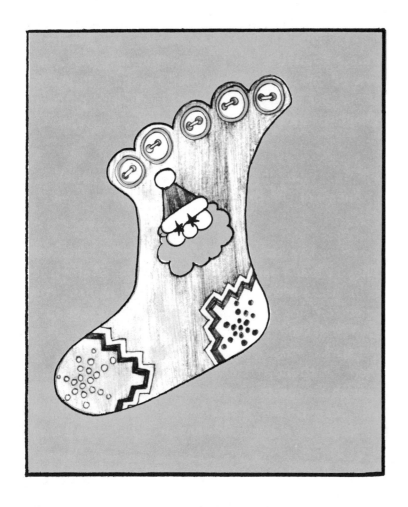

the mixture stands in firm, meringue-like peaks. Then drift the "snow" onto the greenery by scooping up handfuls of suds and brushing them over the branches.

Place a heap of snowballs, and a snowman, too, under the tree, on the mantel, or in the center of your Christmas party table. Make a "snow" mixture, but this time keep adding soap until it is as stiff as dough. Dip your hands into water, and form snowballs. Keep packing until you have a large ball, a medium-sized ball, and a small one. Place on top of one another to form a typical snowman. Press candy, raisins or buttons into the face for features, and tie a piece of cloth around the "neck" for a scarf.

12. Thread strings of popcorn or cranberries to drape around the tree. You might like to use both, alternating one popcorn, then one cranberry, or putting them in whatever order pleases you. After Christmas you can take these off your tree and drape them on bushes out-of-doors, for the winter birds to eat.

13. Dip macaroni (any or all of the wonderful shapes available—shell, stars, wagon wheels, bow ties, elbows) in bowls of food coloring, spread on newspaper to dry, then string in colorful patterns. They will look nice draped 'round the tree, too!

14. Attach lots of lollipops (by their sticks) to branches of the tree, with bright ribbon bows.

Sparkly Stick Stars brighten a tree, too. They're made of toothpicks or cotton swab sticks. Four sticks are needed for each star. Dip the ends or cotton tips of the sticks in paint, and let them dry. Add a bit of rubber cement in the center of the sticks, cross them on top of one another, and then tie them at the center with thread (leave enough thread to attach each star to a branch of the tree). Brush rubber cement along the length of the sticks, and sprinkle on glitter. That's all there is to it!

These sparkly Christmas stars can also be fastened on a package as part of a festive gift wrap.

For their Christmas party, Shari told how to have some fun with food:

15. Serve "snowballs" (balls of vanilla ice cream sprinkled with shredded coconut) and No-Cook Candy. Just chop one cup each of walnuts, seedless raisins, pitted dates. Mix together thoroughly. Add two tablespoons of honey, and blend it all well. Butter your hands, and roll little balls of the mixture. Then roll each ball in ground

nuts (on waxed paper—just spread one-half cup of ground nuts, and roll the little ball about in it).

16. For table decoration (and for the fun of it!) use marshmallows as building blocks, stick them together with toothpicks, and make Marshmallow Christmas Trees and Snowmen. Here's how:

Place the first marshmallow flat side down, to serve as the wide trunk of the tree. Wet your toothpicks before sticking them into the marshmallows. This makes them easier to insert. Brace a wet toothpick, half in this "trunk" marshmallow, and half in another marshmallow, which is standing on its side directly on top of the trunk. Stick three wet toothpicks halfway into the second marshmallow. One should be sticking out on each side, and one on top. In this way, build your marshmallow tree.

The lowest branch of this tree is three marshmallows wide. Into the marshmallow at the very top of the tree, put a toothpick so that just about one-half inch sticks out. Paste two small silver or gold gummed stars, back to back (sticky sides together) over this piece of toothpick. The little marshmallows are fun, too, for building churches or igloos. Try using cubes of sugar for constructing buildings and walls. Layers of corn syrup will hold these sugar "bricks" in place. You need no instructions for making the marshmallow snowman. He's just a fat and funny fellow.

17. Trim the Christmas party table in red and white. Cut a deep fringe along both ends of a pack-age of red crepe paper, while it's still folded. (The fringe should be about three inches deep on each side.) Cover the table itself with a white cloth. Open the package of crepe paper, and place your fringed strip so that it reaches from end to end and hangs down on the sides. Cut off the strip on each side so that it's the same length as the cloth itself.

Shari's youngsters loved playing the Christmas party games. They played them for days before the party, as well as during the festivities:

18. *The Greeting Card Game.* Give each player a pack of four or five old greeting cards, cut into strips about one inch wide. Strips should be well mixed. At a signal, players begin to assemble the strips into original cards—jigsaw puzzle style. The first person to put together all his cards wins. For the next game, the cards in each pack are shuffled once again, the players exchange packs, and the game is repeated.

19. *The Indoor Snowball Fight*. Each child gets a large white balloon "snowball." Everybody inflates his balloon and stands against a wall. One at a time, each player releases his balloon, and as the air escapes, the "snowballs" flip madly about. Each player then stands on the spot where his snowball landed. The person who has "thrown his snowball" farthest is the winner.

20. Play some jingle bell games:

Jingle Bell Treasure Hunt. Tie a tiny red bow on each jingle bell and hide a number of them around the room. Put a green bow on three bells and hide them, too. These "lucky" bells are worth five points, the others, one point each. Count score after a five-minute hunt. (Little bits of wool make fine bows on these jingle bells.)

Jingle Bell Hot Potato. A jingle bell is passed from player to player as they sit in a circle. Someone sings "Jingle Bells" (What else?) and when the singer abruptly stops, the person holding the bell (or the one who drops it) is out. This continues until there is a final winner.

Thread a Jingle Relay. Dip one end of two long pieces of thin string into nail polish and allow to dry. Tie a knot at the other end of each string. Put thirty jingle bells in a big box. Divide the group into two teams, and let each team member add two jingles, and pass the string to the next in line.

21. *Box to Box*. Here's a game that uses the bottom halves of big empty gift boxes (large enough to step into). Place boxes across the room so that they form a path. (Because boxes can slip and slide on the floor, *do* be careful. If your room has no rug, place a strip of double-faced tape under each box.) Each player takes his turn at walking, stepping only in the boxes. When a player steps out of a box by accident, or falls, he or she is out. (This is an exciting relay game, too—make two box paths, and divide the players into two teams.)

22. *Pack Santa's Sack*. This is a quiet game, but a very interesting one. Each person gets at least one old magazine and a paper bag. Then everyone has five minutes to leaf through the pages and tear out pictures of likely objects for Santa to carry in his sack. The player who has the greatest number of "gift" pictures in his paper bag is the winner.

23. *"I-Helped-Santa-Pack-His-Sack-and-In-It-I-Put . . ."* The first player says this sentence and then names a toy or gift beginning with the letter A. The next contestant repeats what the first player said, and adds an object starting with B—and so on, through the alphabet, until everyone has had a chance.

24. *The Guessing Tree Game.* As you trim the tree (before the party), count the number of ornaments you hang. As each guest arrives, allow him or her thirty seconds to examine the tree, and write down an estimate of how many doodads there are on the tree. The three closest guesses win.

Hidden Christmas Treasures

During their Christmas vacation, Shari and her youngsters turned to the Table of Contents for ideas. Here's what they found:

—God's Eyes (page 58), which they wove and hung on the Christmas tree.

—How to empty eggs (page 12). They then glued sequins and glitter and loops of string or wool onto the empty eggs, and hung *them* on the Christmas tree.

—Charlie's "Magic Rabbit" trick (page 69). They made some unusual greeting cards using this idea.

—A Christmas treat for winter birds (page 86).

—Totem poles to be made out of empty gift boxes (page 14).

Look in the Table of Contents for yourself. Can you find any Hidden Christmas Treasures that Shari missed?

May I Suggest?

(A guide for parents, teachers and group leaders to the crafts, activities and games in The Tell It—Make It Book)

I find children to be relatively consistent: A good activity one day will generally prove to be good on another. However, a good activity becomes an exciting one—an achievement—when it is bounced off the springboard of the perfect mood and moment.

Sensing the need, and being able to satisfy it—I think that is the secret to Scout troops that go on for years, to classrooms where the room tone is eagerness rather than tension, and to homes where the TV set gets turned off occasionally because the youngsters "have something better to do."

Unfortunately, this is a much more difficult task than it may seem, for those "moods and moments" can be stimulated by so many things—

season, location, available materials, a specific personal or local event, popular TV shows, curriculum, or even the particular interplay of personalities within your group.

This reference chapter is designed to help you find within this book activities that will satisfy both you and your youngsters under a number of circumstances.

First of all, since the seasons roll around with satisfying regularity, may I suggest—?

For Autumn

—"Strictly for the Birds" (page 77) tells the trick of making treats for winter birds.

—For Halloween activities see "The Wildest Indian" for the Mask (page 23). Indian Headdresses (page 21), and the Sock Hobbyhorse (page 23), which can be ridden by a small cowboy as he makes his trick-or-treat rounds.

For Winter

The early part of winter seems to be dominated by Thanksgiving and Christmas, the second half by a series of respiratory ailments. Let me deal with all three.

—Thanksgiving. "The Wildest Indian" (page 11) describes many activities keyed to the American Indian.

—Christmas. In addition to the twenty-four projects in "How-Many-Days-'til-Christmas?" (page 93), "Hidden Christmas Treasures" (page 107) suggests other items in the book which are adaptable for Christmas.

—Sick-in-Bed Play.

The weaving of God's Eyes (using cotton swab sticks, rather than twigs) is a lovely quiet activity. See "Grandma's Sweater," Part 2 (page 58).

"I'll See Me in My Dreams," Part 2 (page 41), involves Hush Puppy in bed with a cold, making hand-shadows on his bedroom wall with a flashlight.

The Indian village can be created by a child seated in bed, because it's all self-contained, constructed inside the lid of a big gift box. That's to be found in "The Wildest Indian," Part 2 (page 11).

—Valentine's Day

The loveliest Valentine gift I ever got from my child came via Miss Judy Albert, third grade teacher at Hawthorne School in Beverly Hills. It's my daughter's silhouette, and the technique is described in "I'll See Me in My Dreams," Part 3 (page 46).

In "How-Many-Days-'til-Christmas?" see Items 2, 3, 4, 5, 6, 7 (pages 96-97) for pleasant and textural ways to make Valentine cards; Item 10 (page 98) for a felt heart which can hold a small gift or card; Item 15 (page 101) for homemade Valentine candy, otherwise known as "No-Cook Candy."

For Spring

—Easter. At Eastertime, eggs are inescapable. We blow them empty, and do some unusual decorations and an egg puppet in "The Wildest Indian" (page 12).

—For the basic Easter art projects, try pictures of chicks, rabbits, etc., created as described in Items 1 and 5 in "How-Many-Days-'til-Christmas?" (pages 94, 97).

—Spring suggests flowers and plantings. "Lamb Chop's Green Thumb," Part 1 (page 27) and Part 2 (page 32), deals with easy, novel techniques for making your garden—anywhere—and watching it grow.

—Mother's Day and Father's Day. Silhouette pictures are welcome gifts for parents ("I'll See Me in My Dreams," Part 3, page 46), as are the original pictures created with textural and unusual materials in Item 1 of "How-Many-Days-'til-Christmas?" (page 94). God's Eyes ("Grandma's Sweater," page 58) make fine wall hangings. To create gift cards that are a little off the beaten path, see Items 2, 3, 4, 5, 6, 7 in "How-Many-Days-'til-Christmas?", Part 2 (pages 96–97).

For Summer

—For outdoor play (backyard, picnic, poolside, campground), see the fun with soapsuds described in "How-Many-Days-'til-Christmas?" (page 98). This is great out-of-doors because when you're all done, the mess can be hosed away. Try making "soap snowballs" and using them for target practice against a handy tree or fence. Soapsuds sculpture is engrossing. Slathering the thick suds all over one another is harmless (if the youngsters are in bathing suits!), and it creates living snowmen.

—I discovered the joys of weaving God's Eyes while on a hike in Griffith Park with a group of Girl Scouts. The senior girls who were leading the hike gave each Brownie a small ball of wool to tuck into her pocket. As they hiked, the children were told to pick up two twigs that appealed to them, with or without leaves. After their meal 'round the campfire, they used these twigs to create God's Eyes. The Scouts saw beautiful results quickly, and were elated. (See "Grandma's Sweater," page 58.)

If You're Giving a Party

—You might like to make your own invitations, using the techniques in Items 2, 3, 4, 5, 6, 7 of "How-Many-Days-'til-Christmas?" (pages 96-97).

—Food, fun and favors are also described in the Christmas chapter. See Items 14, 15, 16, 17, 18 (pages 100–102).

—For games see Items 18, 19, 20, 21, 22, 23, 24, 25, 26. These games are highly switchable—for example, instead of having the guests guess how many ornaments are on the Christmas tree, fill a glass jar or small paper bag with hard candy or pennies, and as each guest comes in, let him make a guess. The winner gets to keep the goodies.

Even the games that are Santa-oriented can be easily changed to suit your purpose. For example, "I-Helped-Santa-Pack-His-Sack-and-In-It-I-Put . . ." can be switched to "I-Came-To-—'s-Party-and-I-Gave-Him (Her)-A-Big-—."

There are also two games in "The Wildest Indian," Part 2 (page 24).

—Craft activities are a fine addition to a party, particularly as the children assemble. Prepare the necessary materials described in Item 1 of "How-Many-Days-'til-Christmas?" (page 94), and let the youngsters create their own pictures as they pile in.

—Themes add color and flavor. If you want to do a Cowboys-and-Indians Party, "The Wildest Indian" has games and crafts that will fill the bill.

If Your Group Wants To Make Puppets

See "The Wildest Indian," Part 2 (page 15) for the Matchbox Puppet, Balloon Puppet, Egg Puppet, and the standard useful draped body.

If You Wish To Put On an Informal Show

—Charlie Horse's magic tricks are "real" magic, and yet very easy to do. See "Charlie Horse's Magic Show," Part 2 (page 69). In addition, the silly show which is such a flop (the entire story of Part 1) can be put on its feet as a playlet, substituting your youngsters for Lamb Chop, Charlie Horse and Hush Puppy. This little playlet should, in my opinion, end with the punchline on page 66 where Charlie Horse proudly tells Shari that he *succeeded* in his disappearing trick—"I made my whole audience disappear!"

—The Matchbox or Egg Puppets combined with the drape body ("The Wildest Indian," Part 2, page 15) are all usable for dramatization.

—The hand shadows in "I'll See Me in My Dreams," Part 2 (Page 41), are very easy, and can be done superbly with the light from a slide or movie projector. The group might enjoy doing "Old McDonald Had a Farm" and taking turns making the animals appear in shadow.

Crafts Which Can Be Given as Gifts

Craft activities where the end product is artistic include—

—God's Eyes ("Grandma's Sweater," Part 2, page 58).

—Item 1 of "How-Many-Days-'til-Christmas?" (page 94).

—The plantings and kitchen cuttings in "Lamb Chop's Green Thumb," Part 1 (page 27) and Part 2 (page 32), are very amusing and attractive once they have taken root.

—The silhouettes of youngsters ("I'll See Me in My Dreams," Part 2 (page 41)) are very giveable.

If You Are Working in the Kitchen

And you'd like the youngsters to play nearby, I suggest—

—The preparation of treats for winter birds in "Strictly for the Birds," Part 1 (page 77) and Part 2 (page 86).

—The planting activities in "Lamb Chop's Green Thumb," Part 1 (page 27) and Part 2 (page 32).

—The pictures created with rice, popcorn, macaroni, puffed cereal, etc., in Item 1, "How-Many-Days-'til-Christmas?" (page 94).

—The Marshmallow Building Blocks in Item 16, "How-Many-Days-'til-Christmas?" (page 101).

If Your Group Is Made Up of
Divergent Free Spirits

Read them the story of "The Wildest Indian," and then let each select his own craft from the many described there. Some are active, some require quiet concentration—a couple are complex, and the others quickly achieved. There is something for everybody in this group project.